LETTER TRACING FOR KIDS

MIA

TRACE MY NAME WORKBOOK

Can't Find Your Name?

Have our elves create a personalized book with the name of your choice today!

VISIT US AT:

PERSONALIZETHISBOOK.COM

Cover and page design by Cool Journals Studios - Copyright 2017

ABOUT ME

MY NAME IS:

Mia

I AM ☐ YEARS OLD.

I LIVE IN:

For parents

For kids

DRAW YOU AND YOUR FAMILY

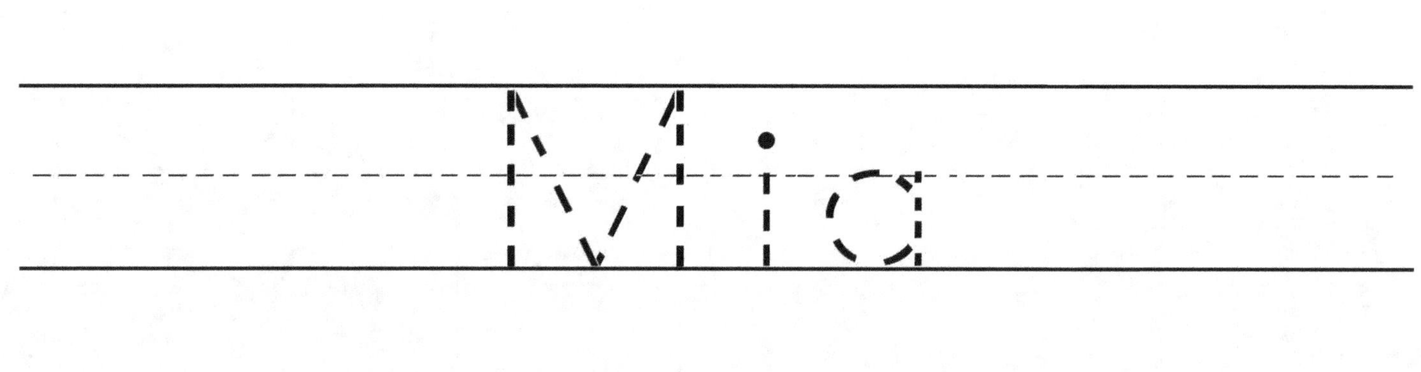

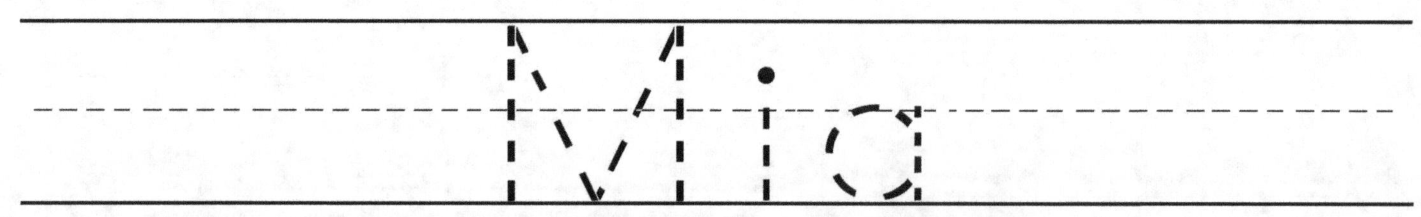

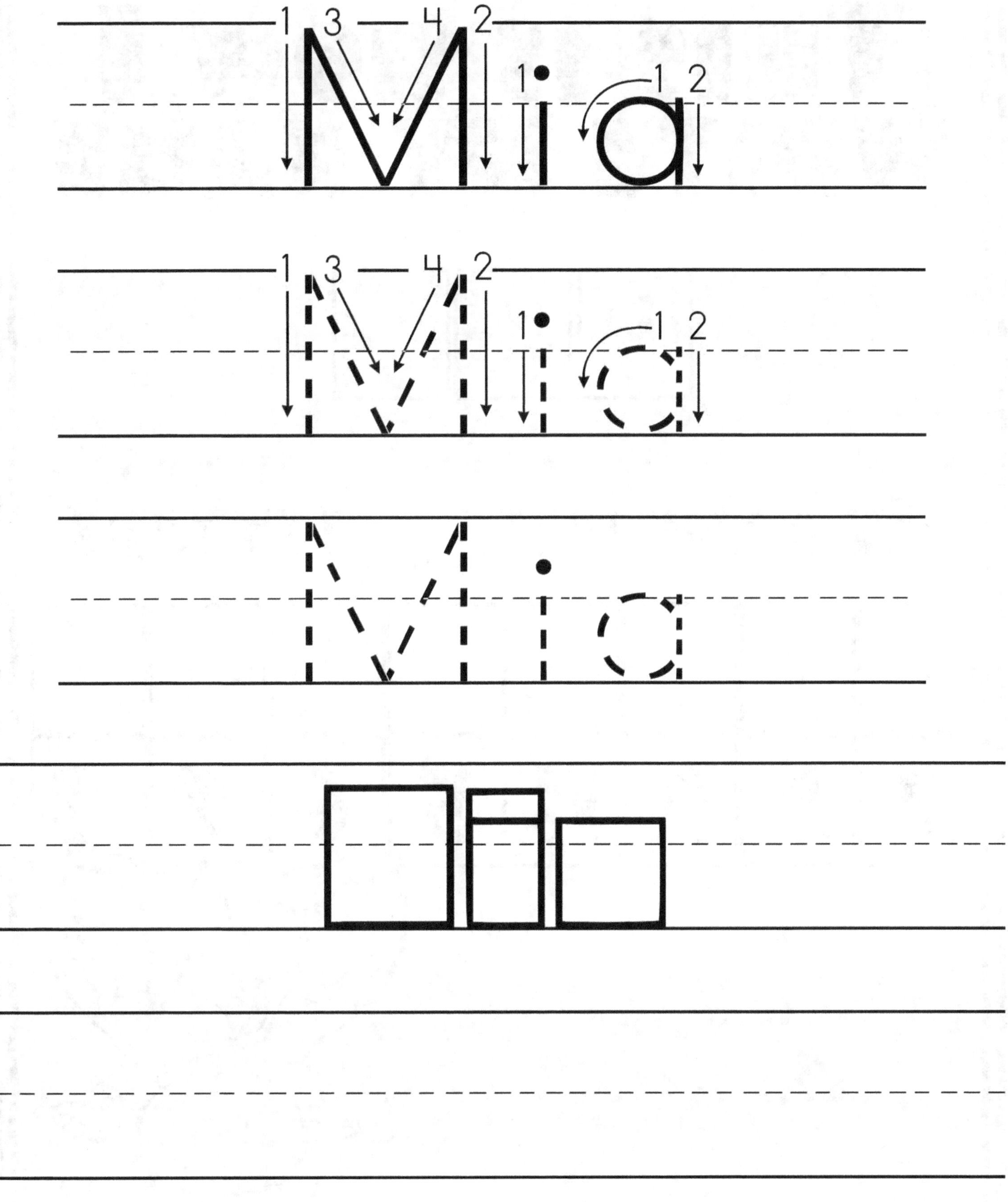

THIS IS HOW I WRITE MY NAME

MY NAME HAS ___ LETTERS

1	2	3	4	5	6	7	8

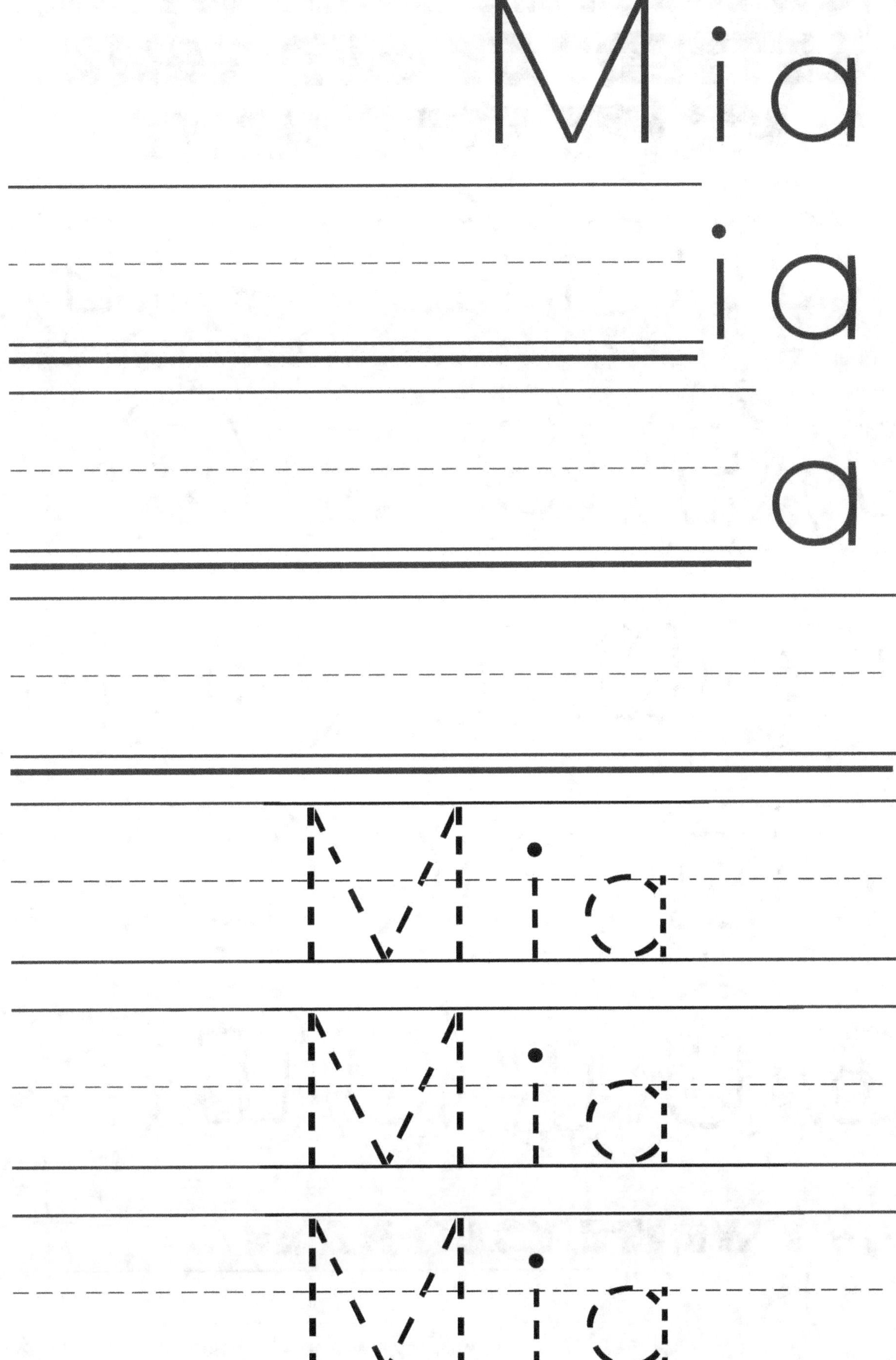

COLOR THE EGGS WITH LETTERS OF OUR NAME WRITE YOUR NAME

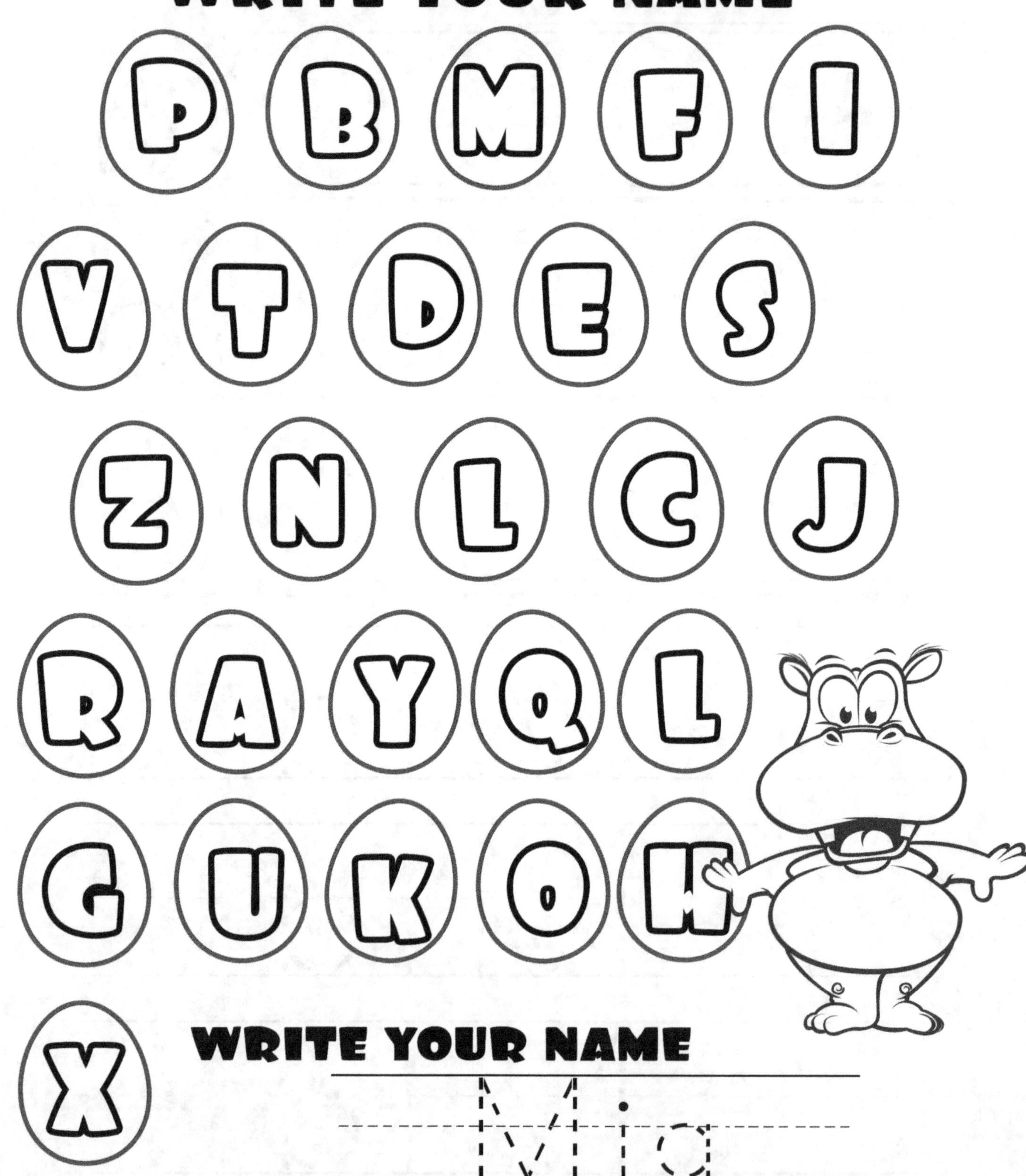

WRITE YOUR NAME

Mia

WRITE YOU NAME WITH.

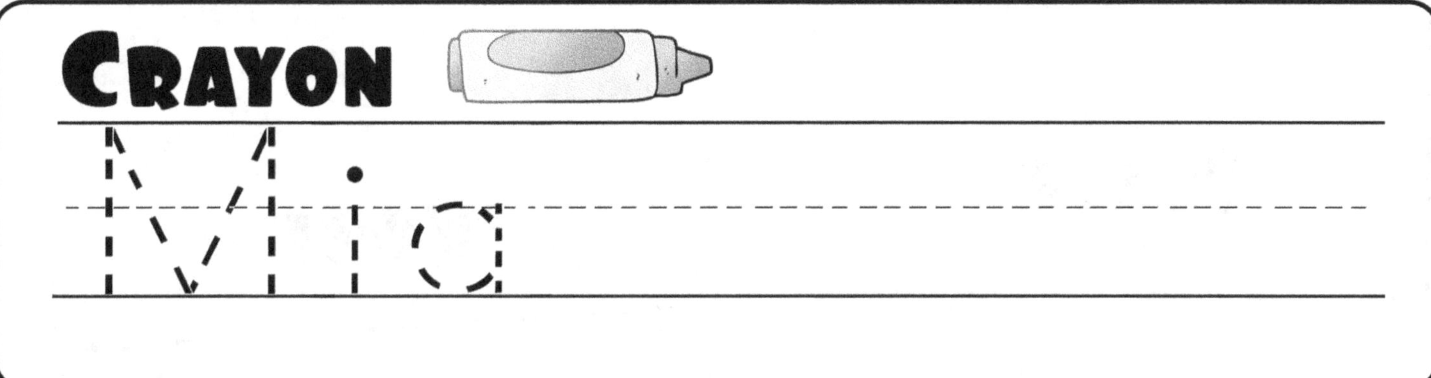

PEN

Mia

CRAYON

Mia

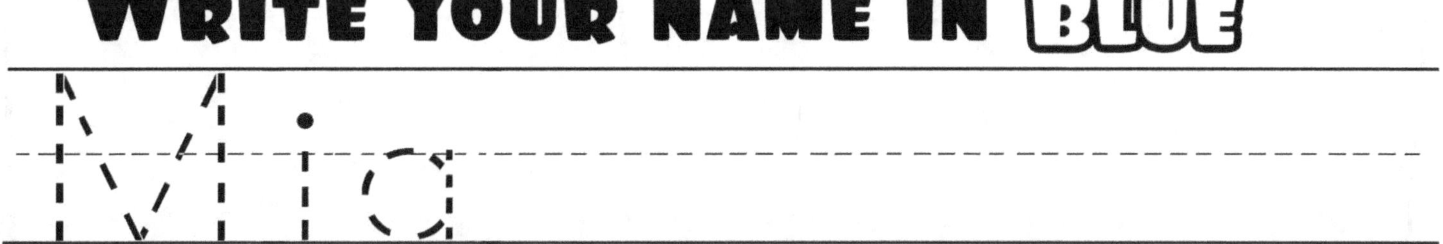

WRITE YOUR NAME IN BLUE

Mia

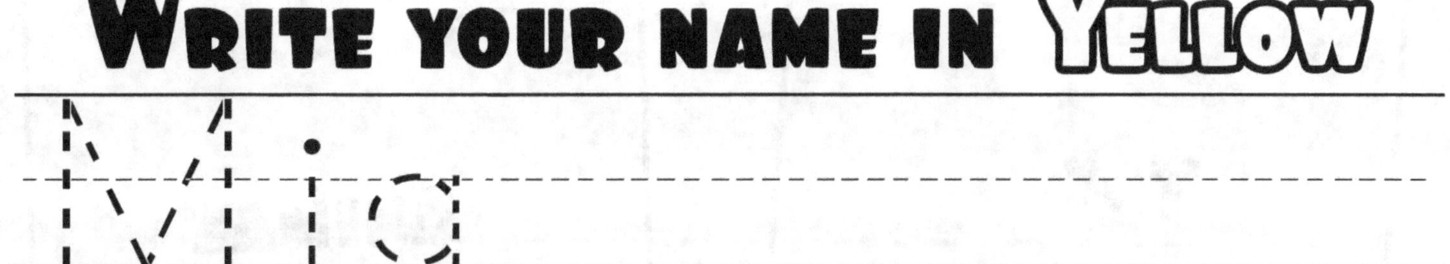

WRITE YOUR NAME IN YELLOW

Mia

DRAW YOUR FAVORITE THINGS

COLOR

FOOD

TOY

ANIMAL

MY NAME

<table>
<tr><td>My name
starts with

________</td><td>My name
ends with

________</td></tr>
</table>

FILL THE LETTERS OF YOUR NAME WHITH DIFFERENT COLORS

P B V F V I T

D E S Z N L C

J R A Y Q K

G U X O H M

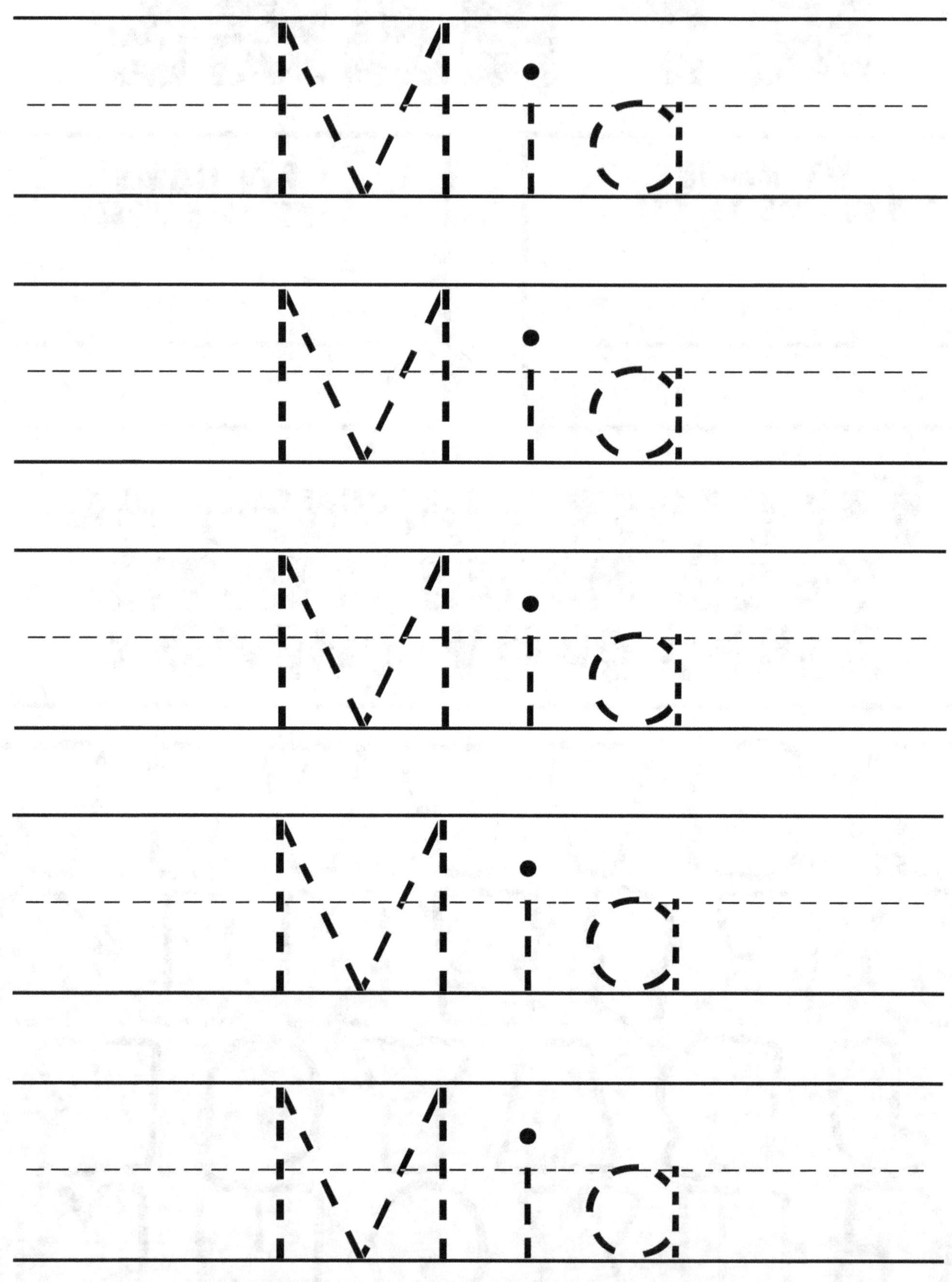

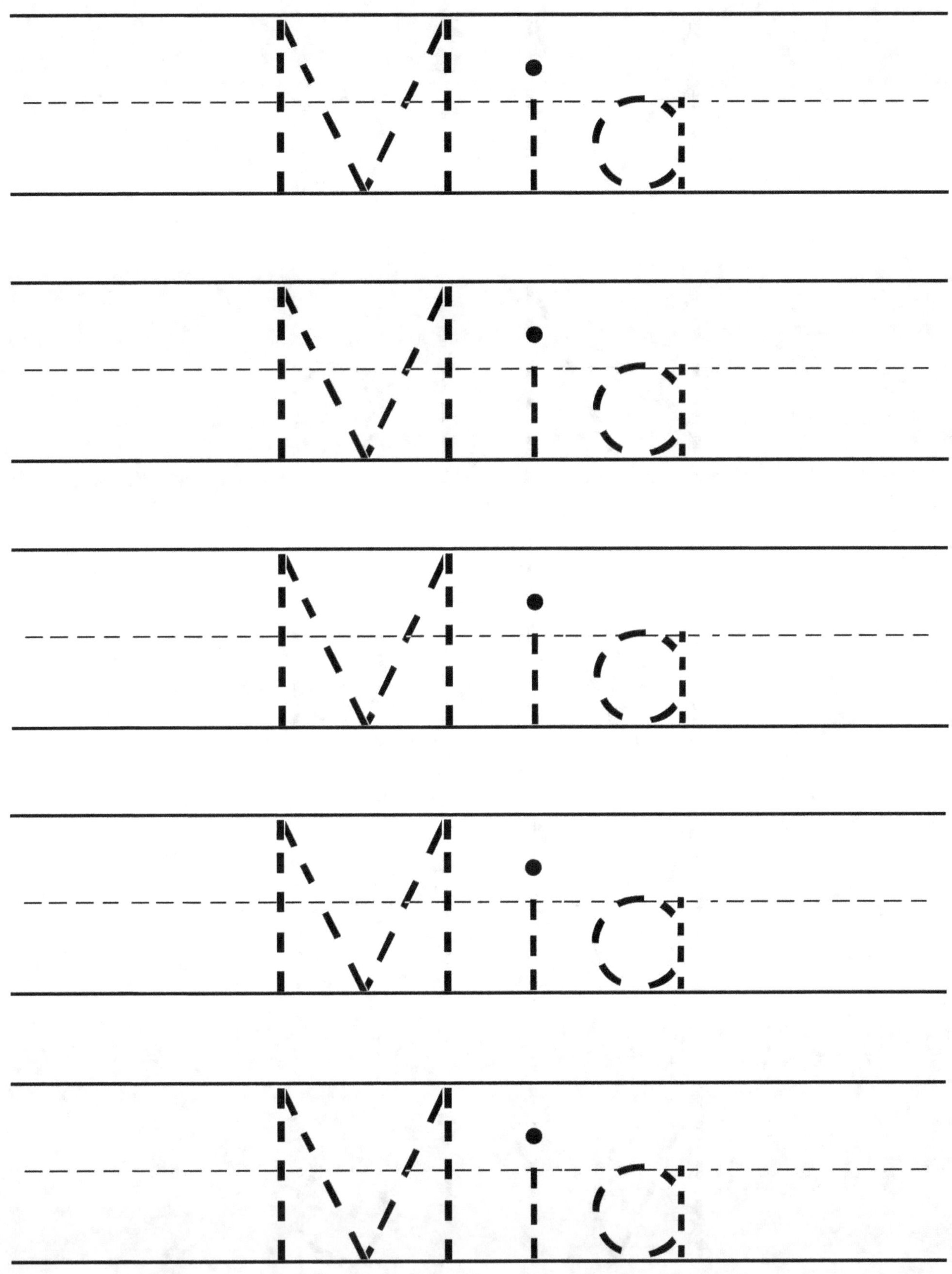

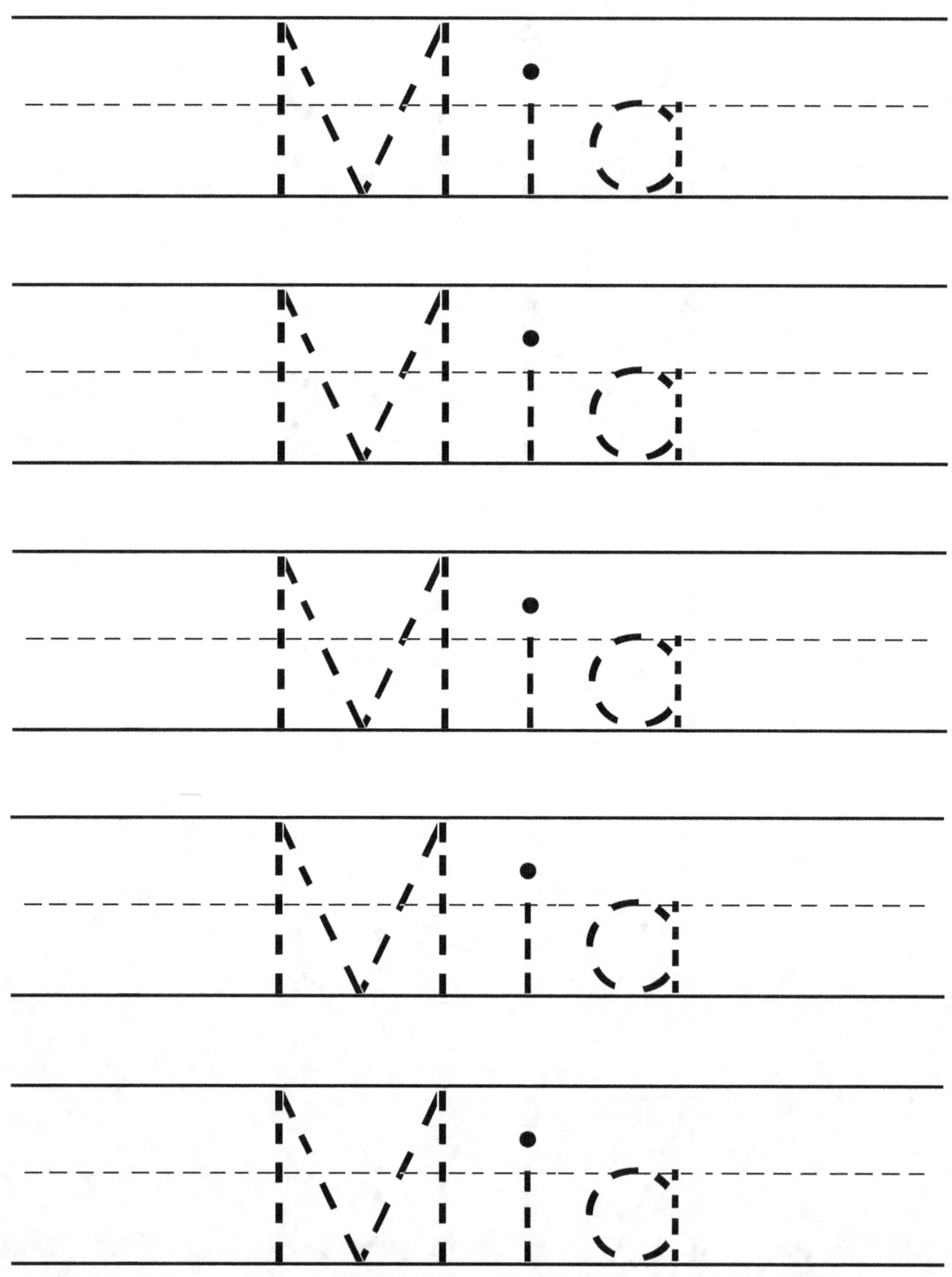

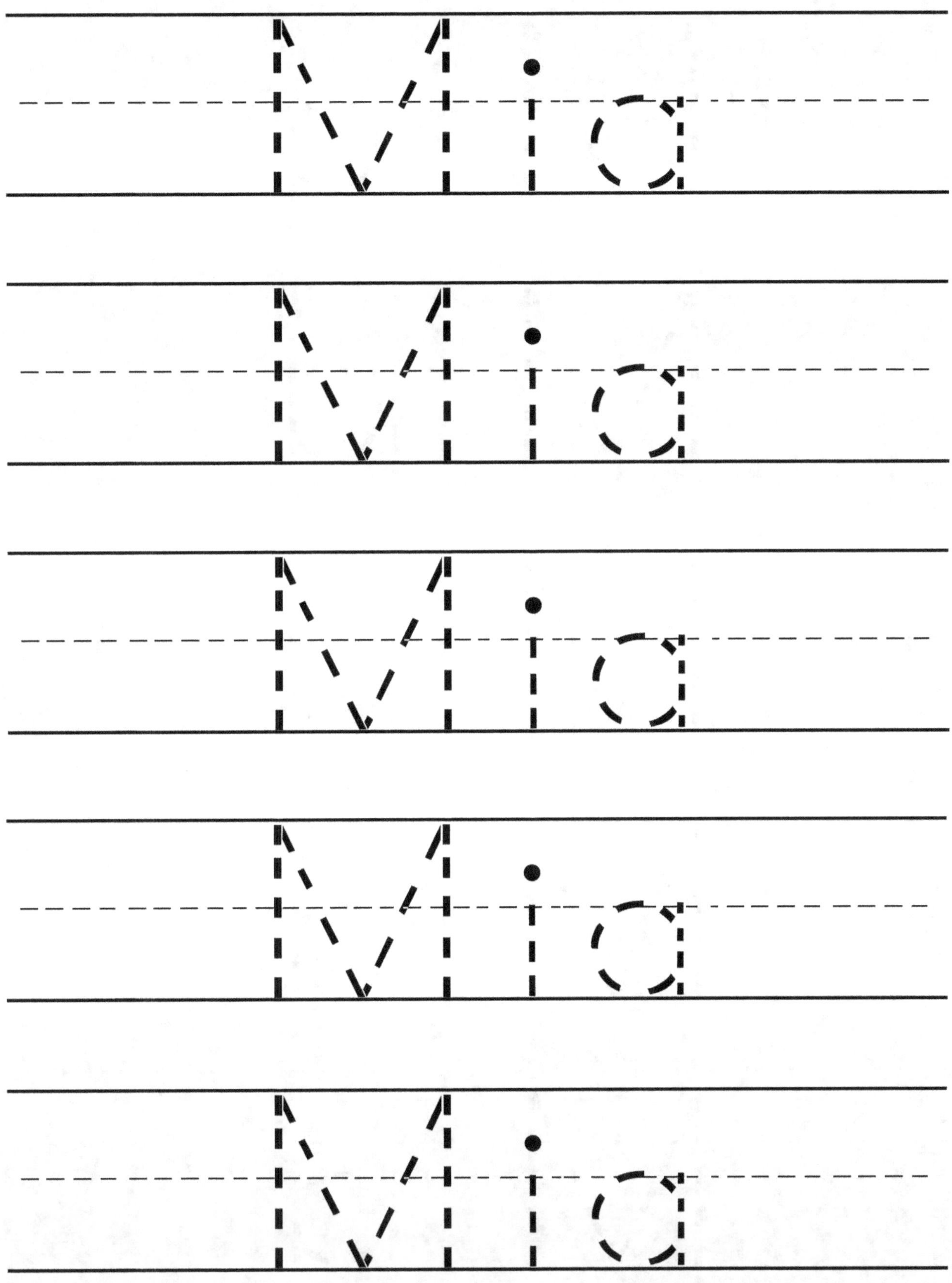

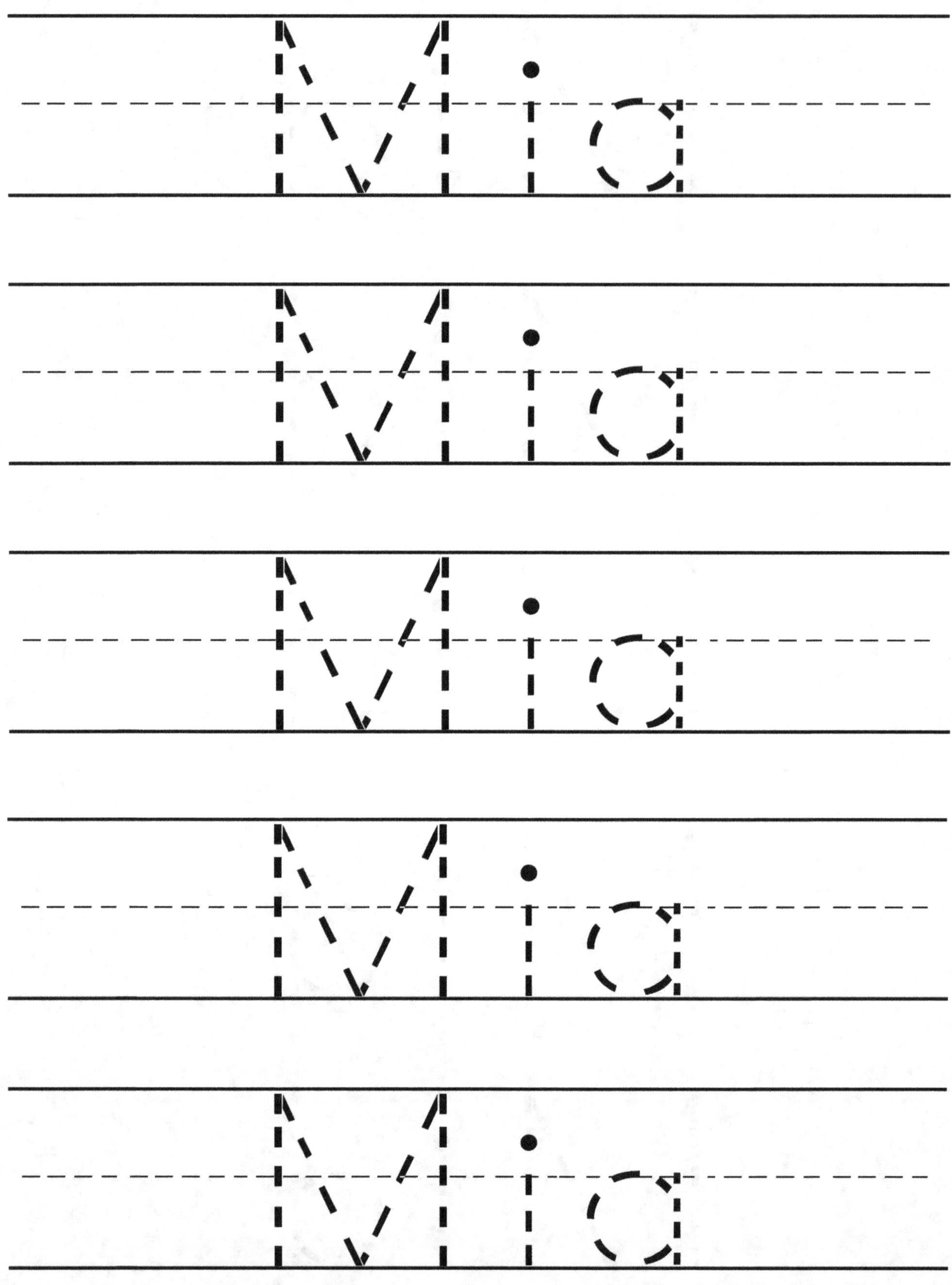

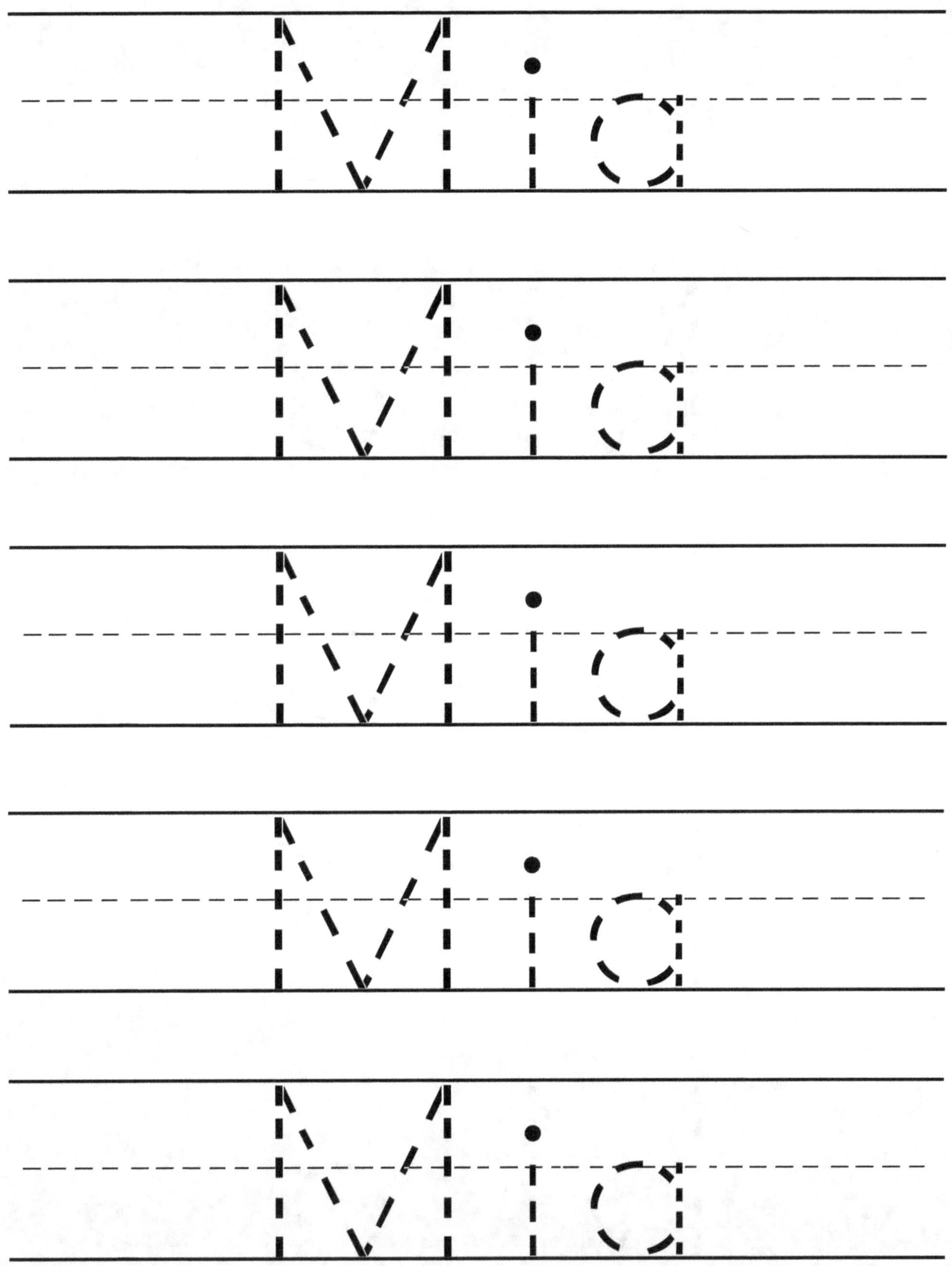

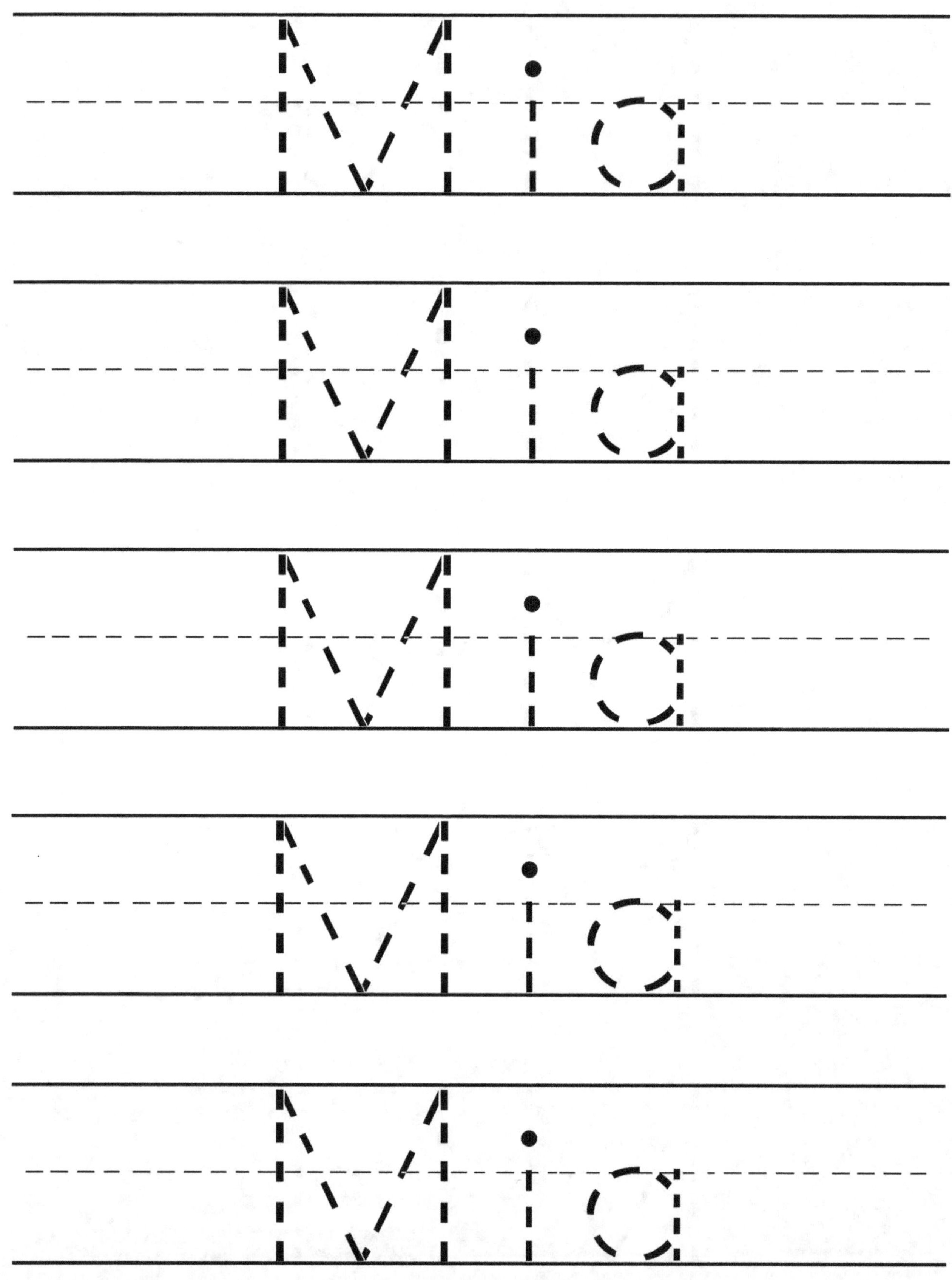

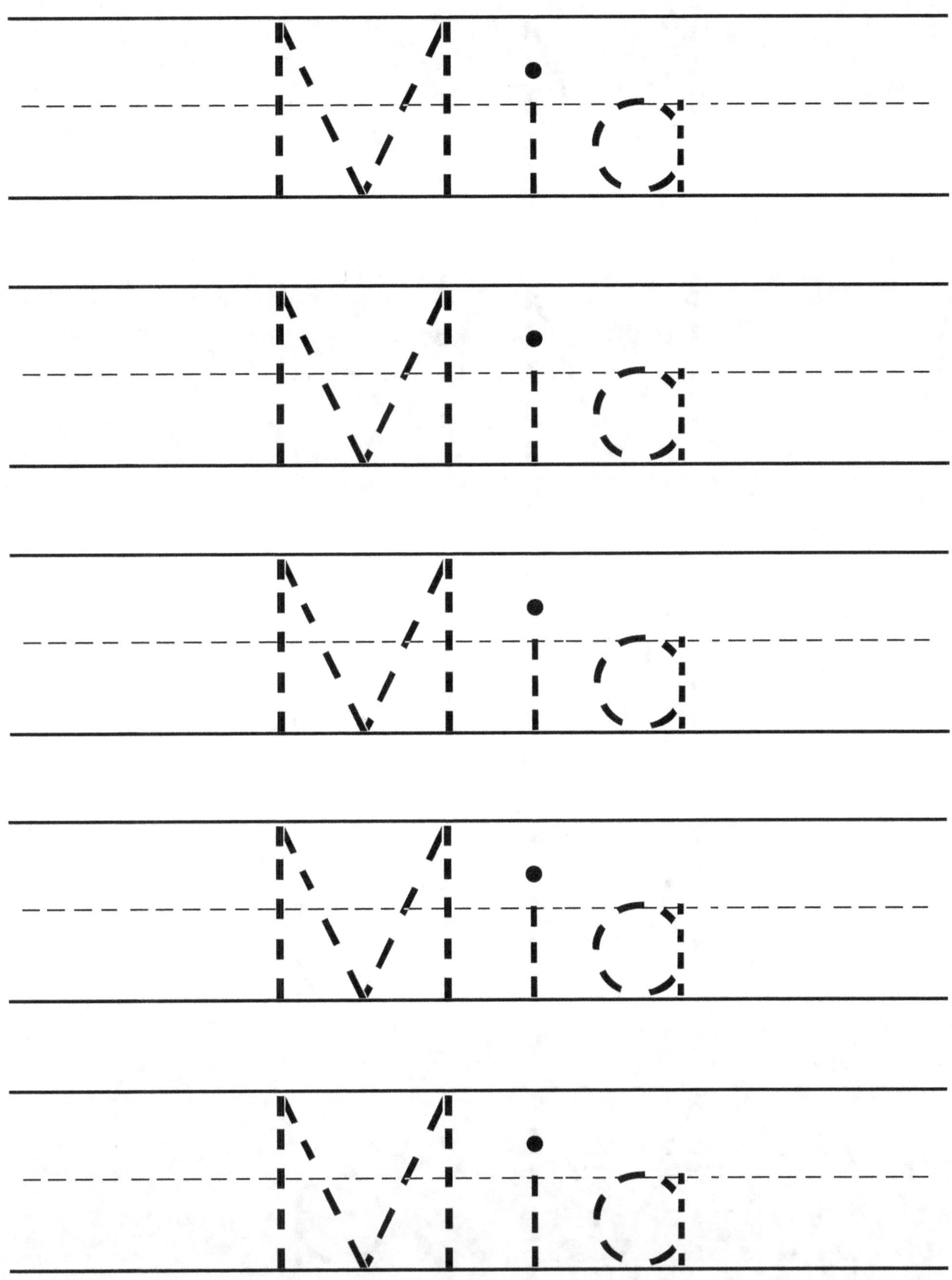

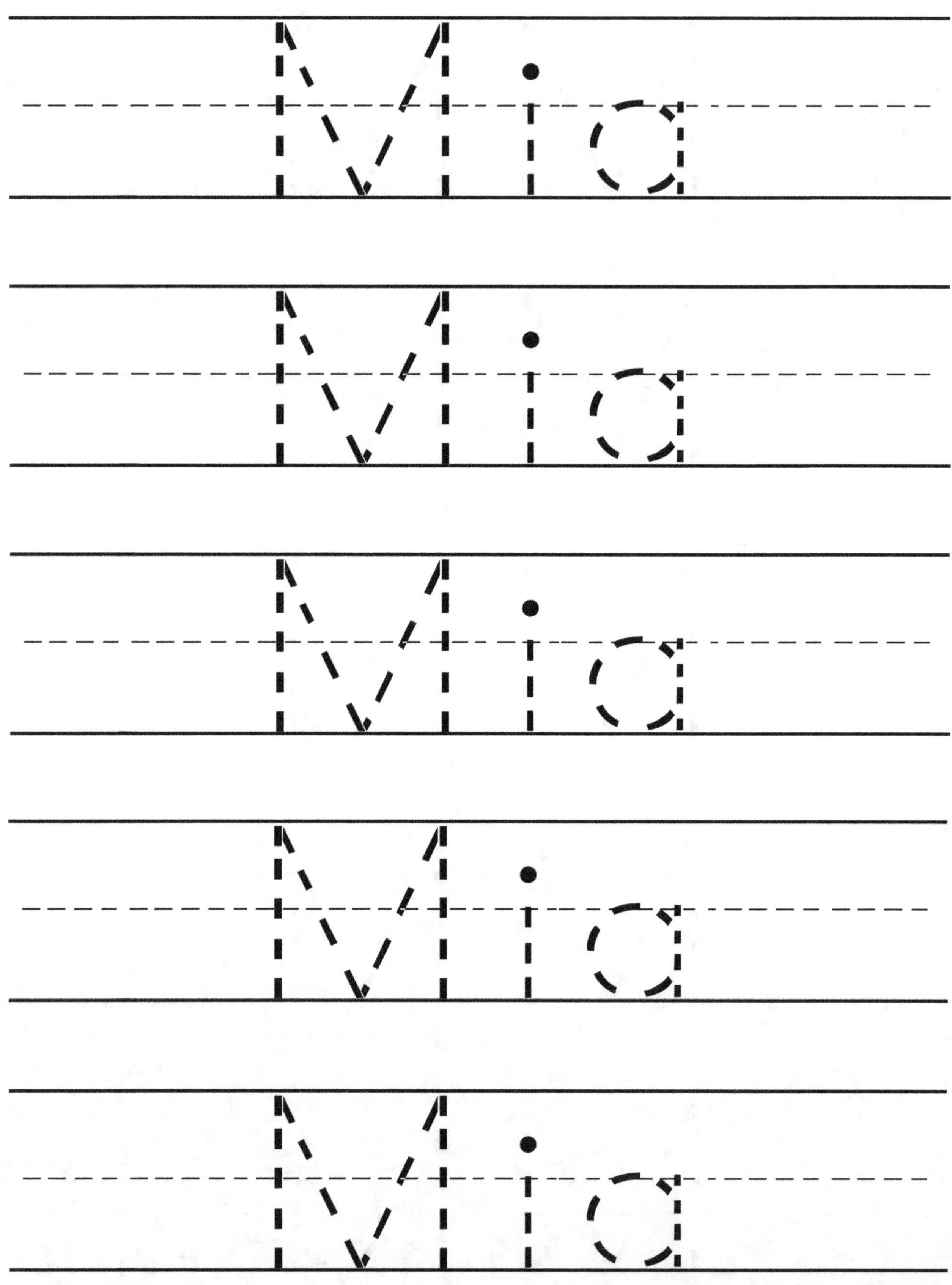

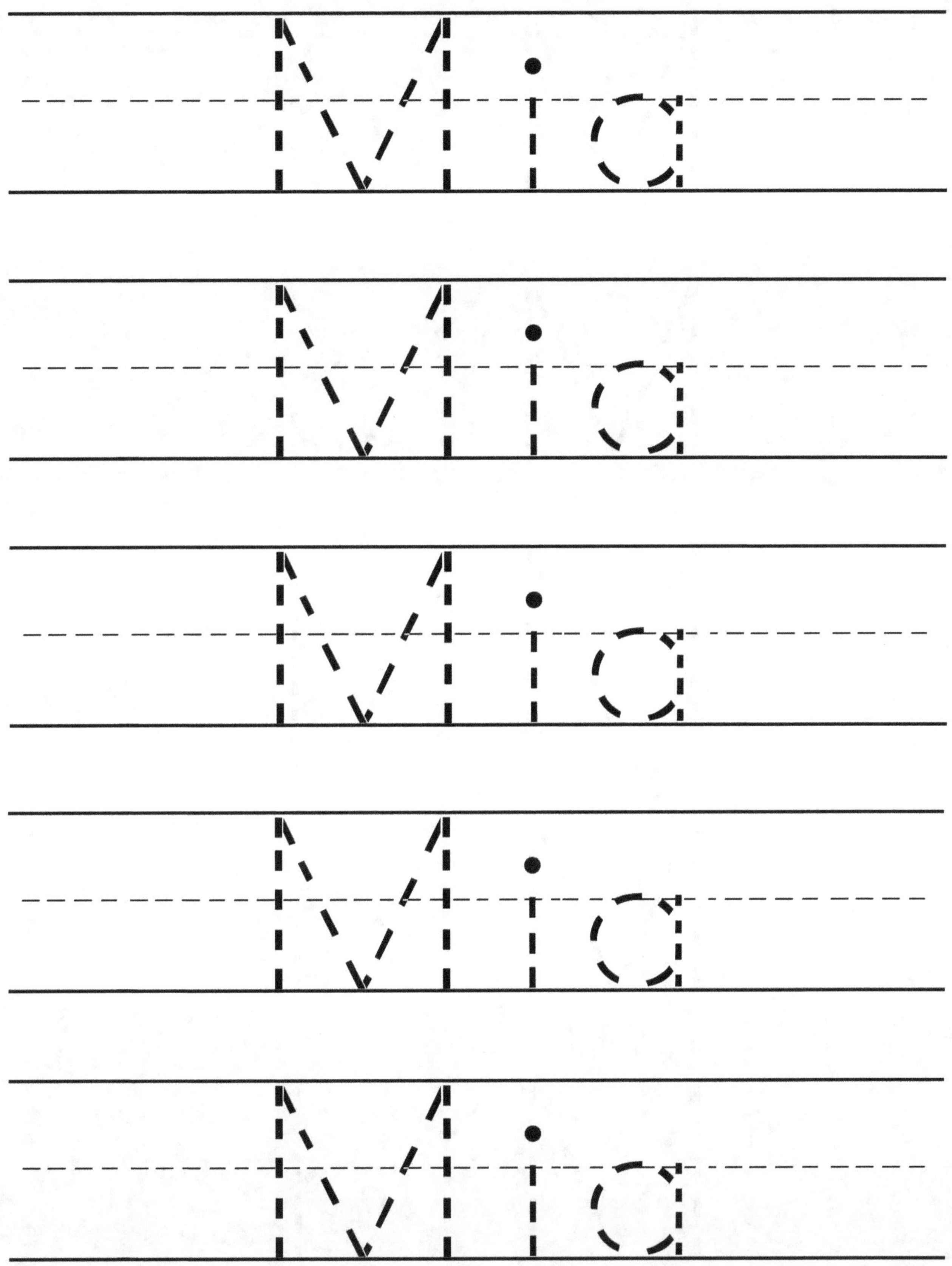

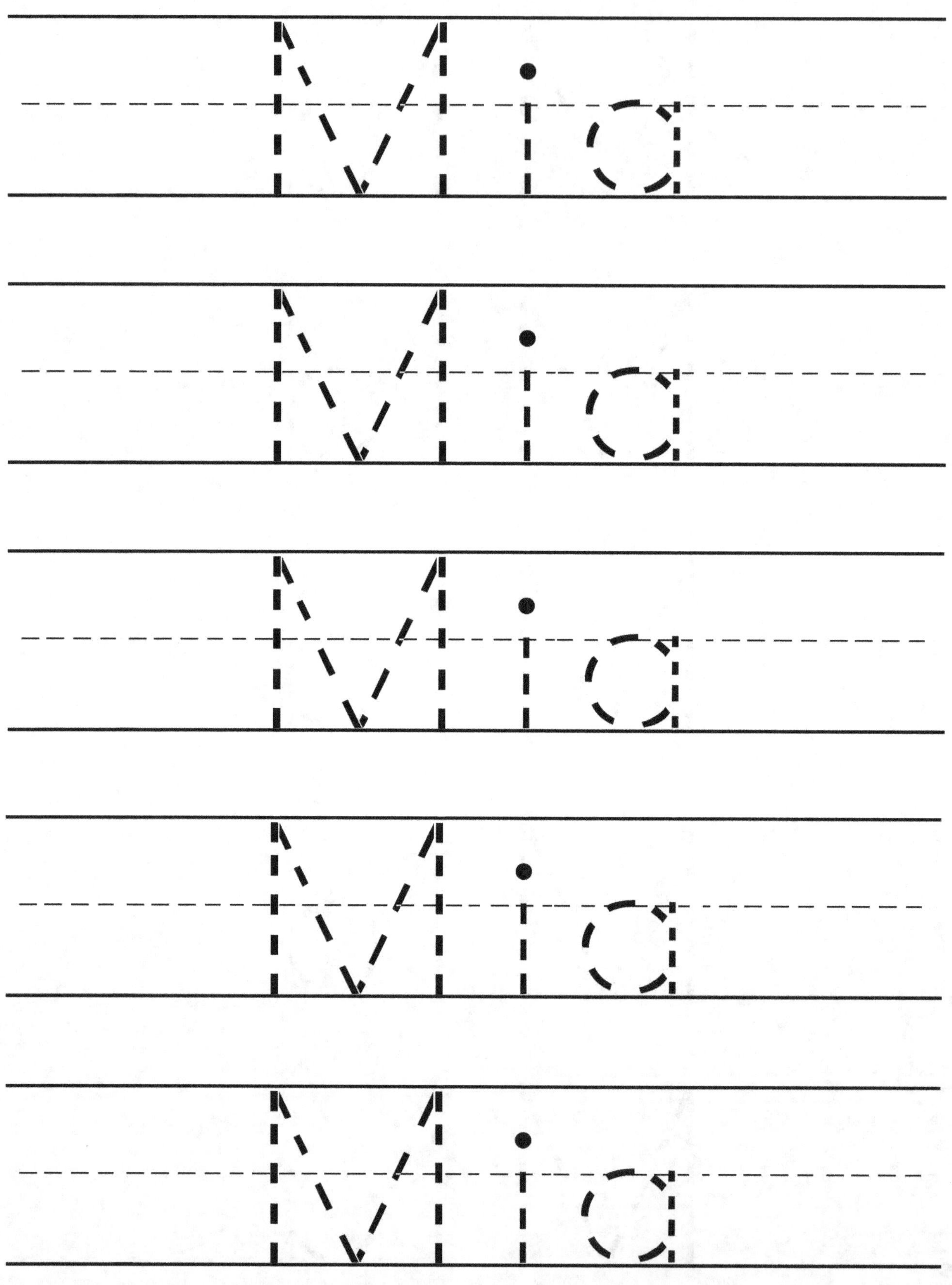

Mia
Mia
Mia
Mia
Mia

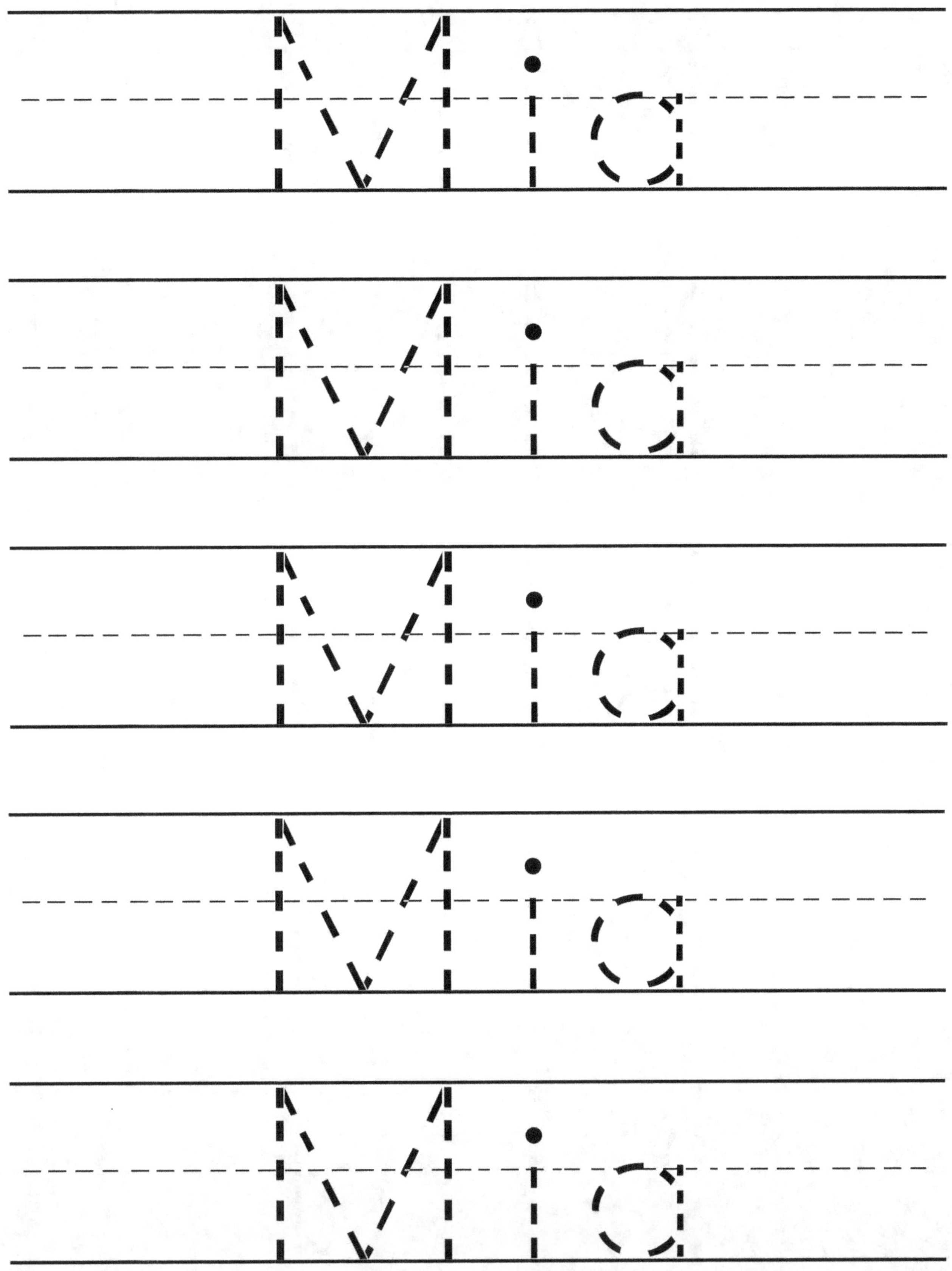

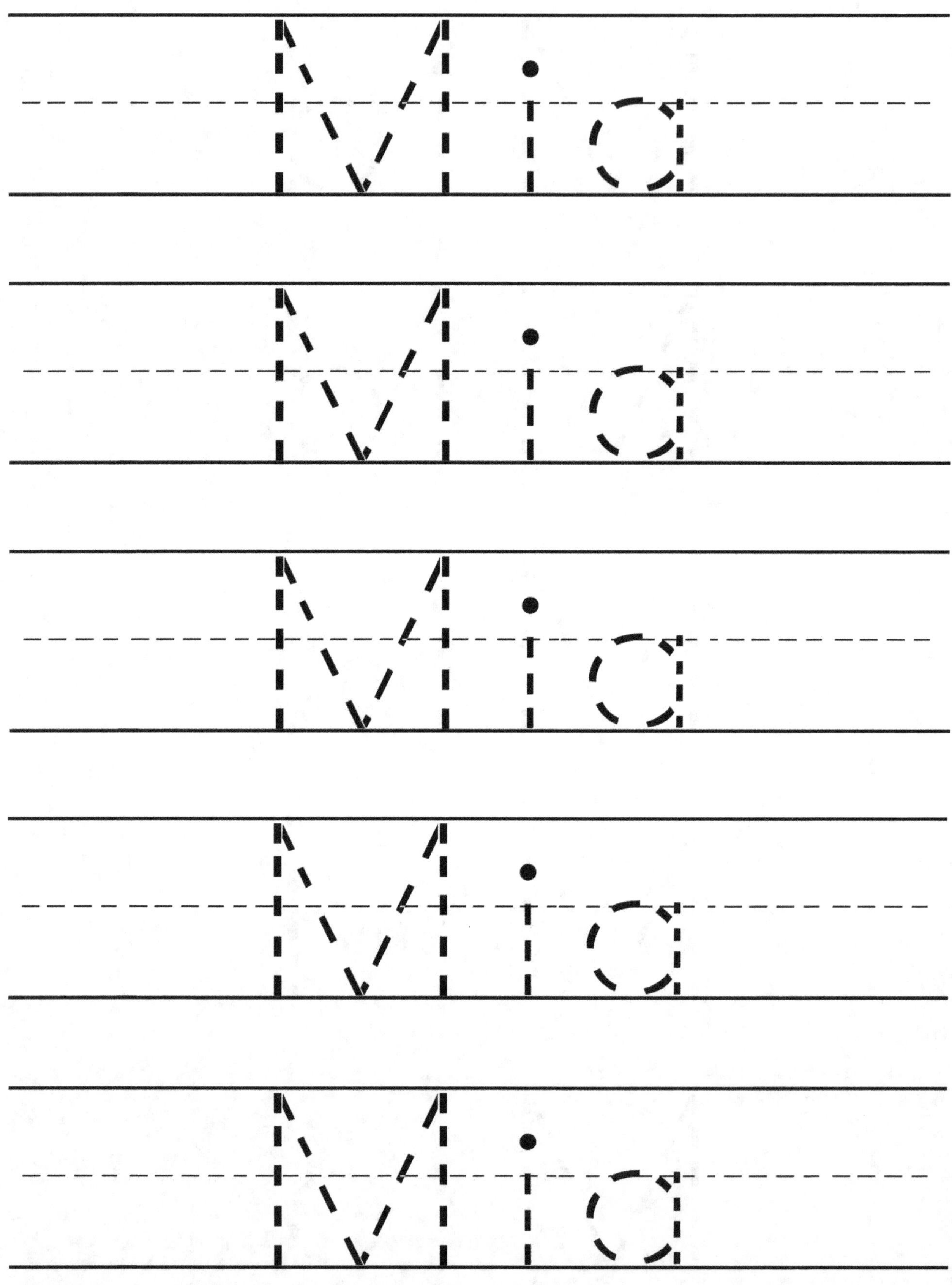

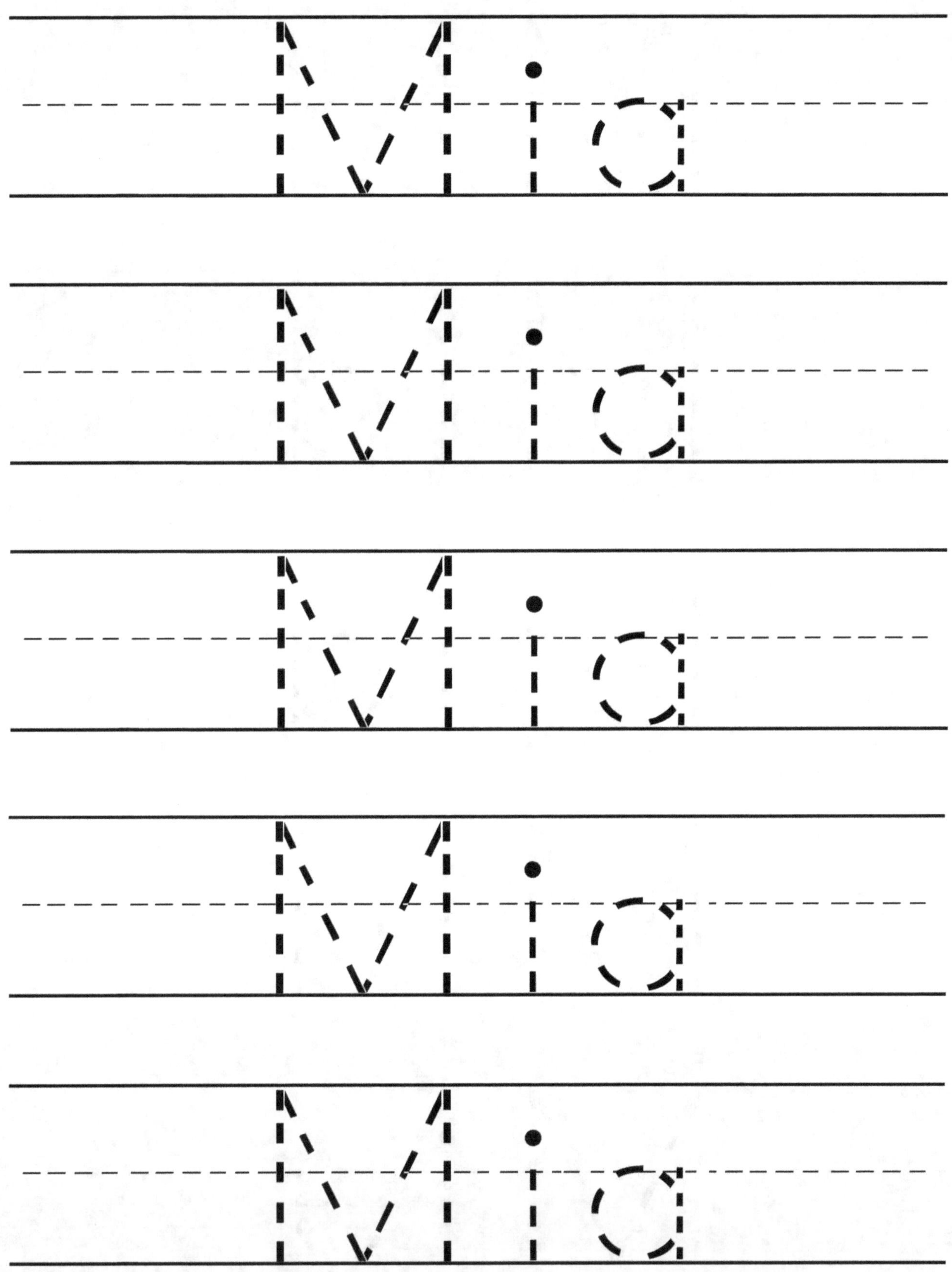

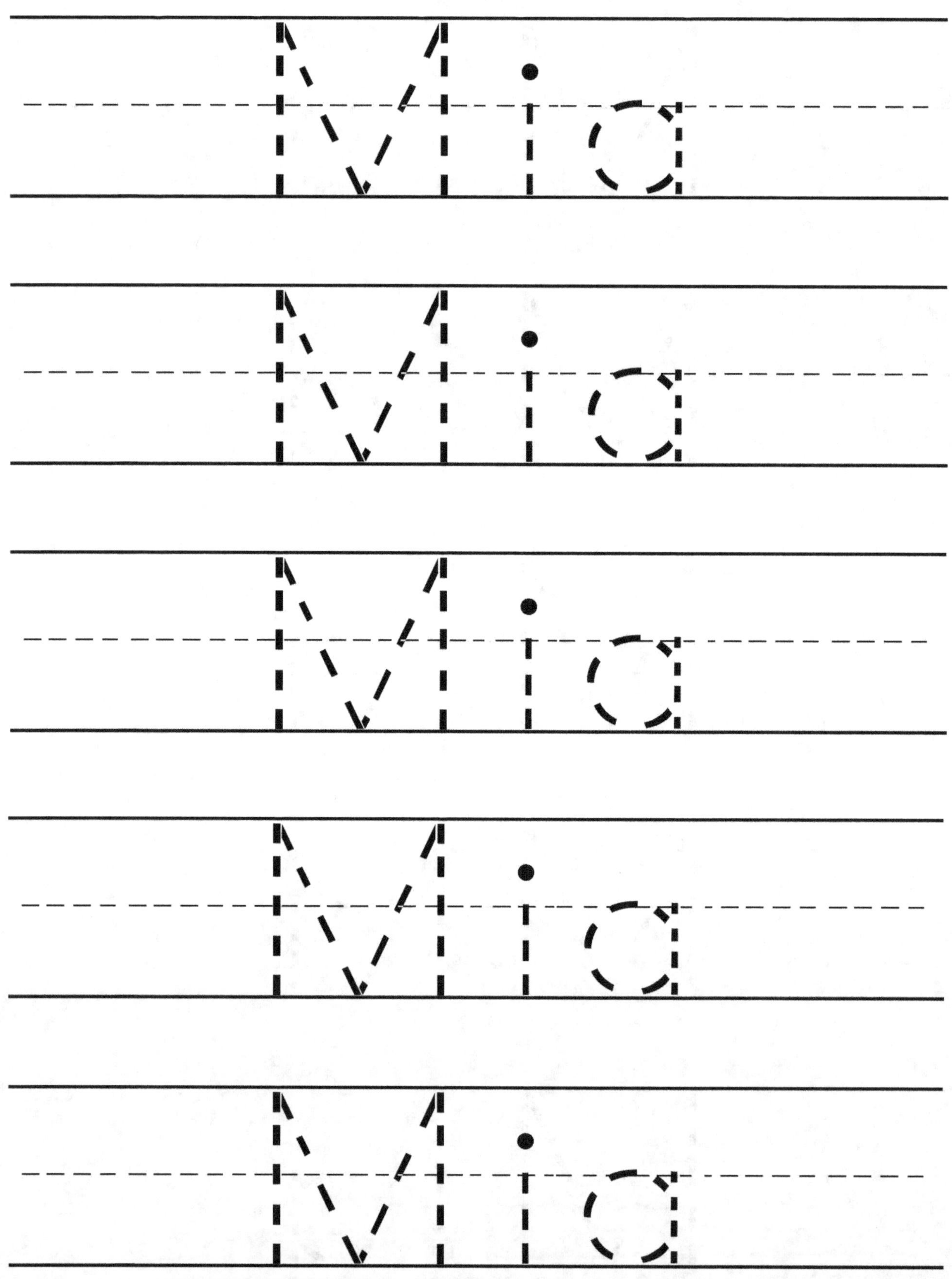

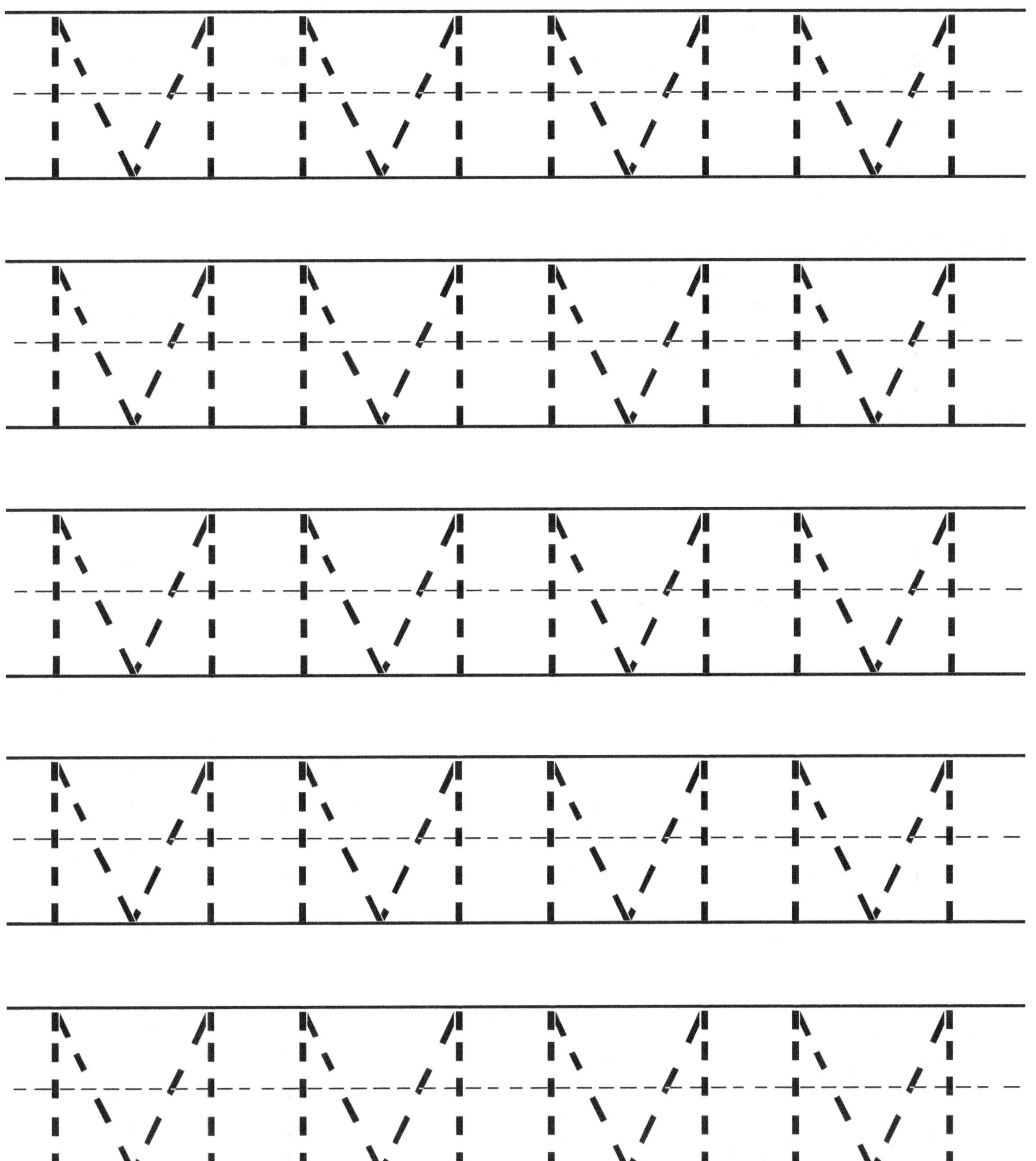

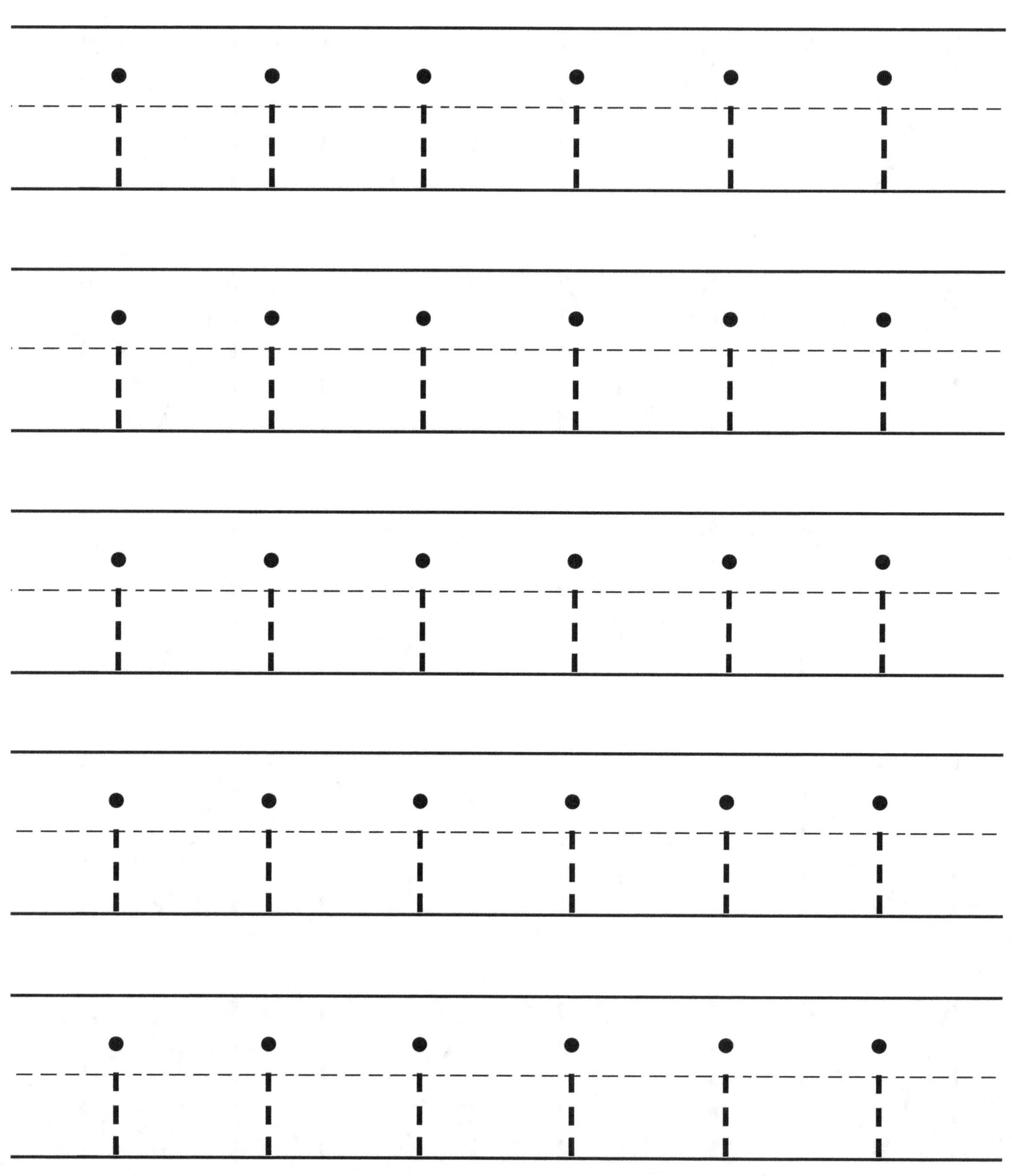

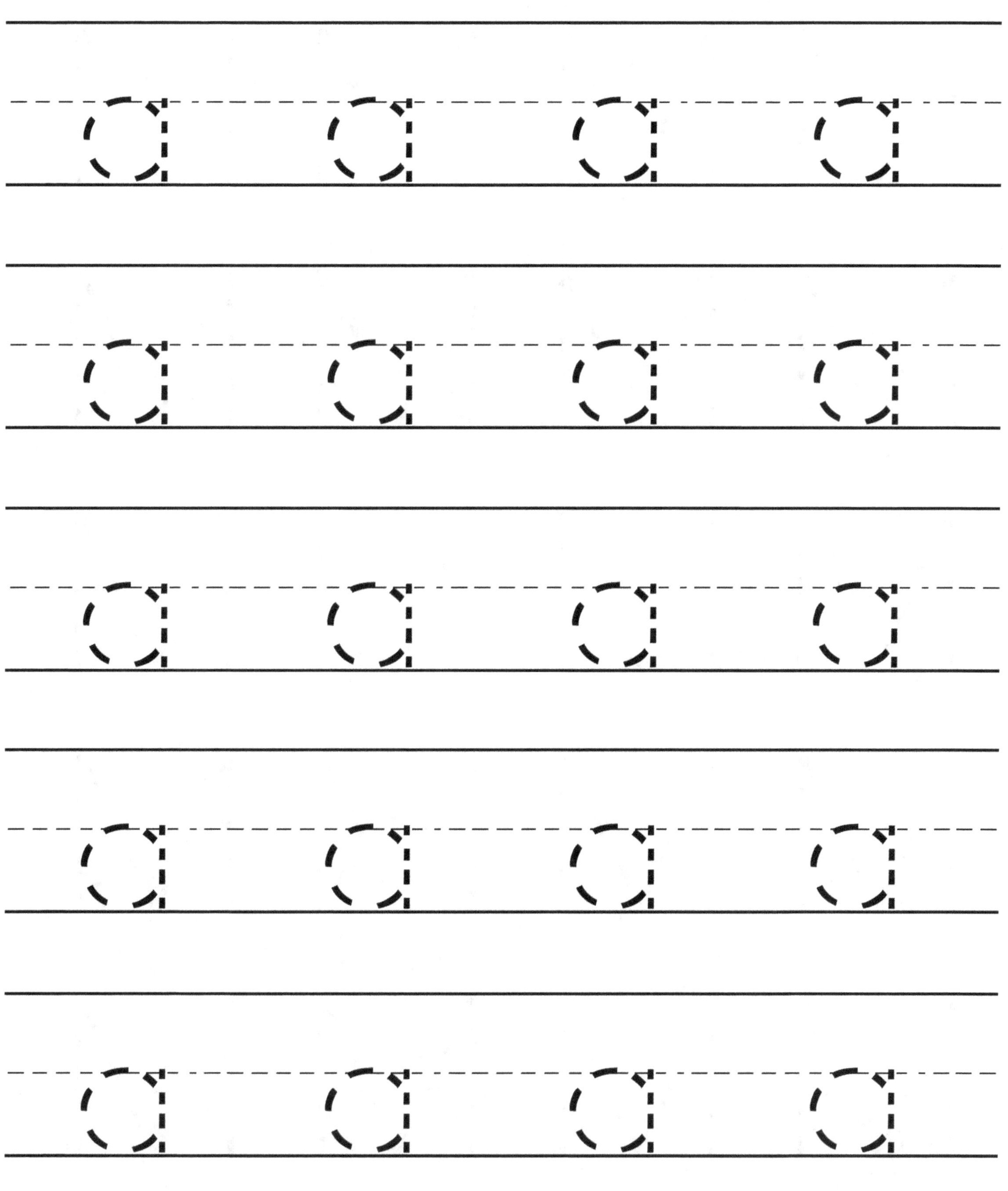

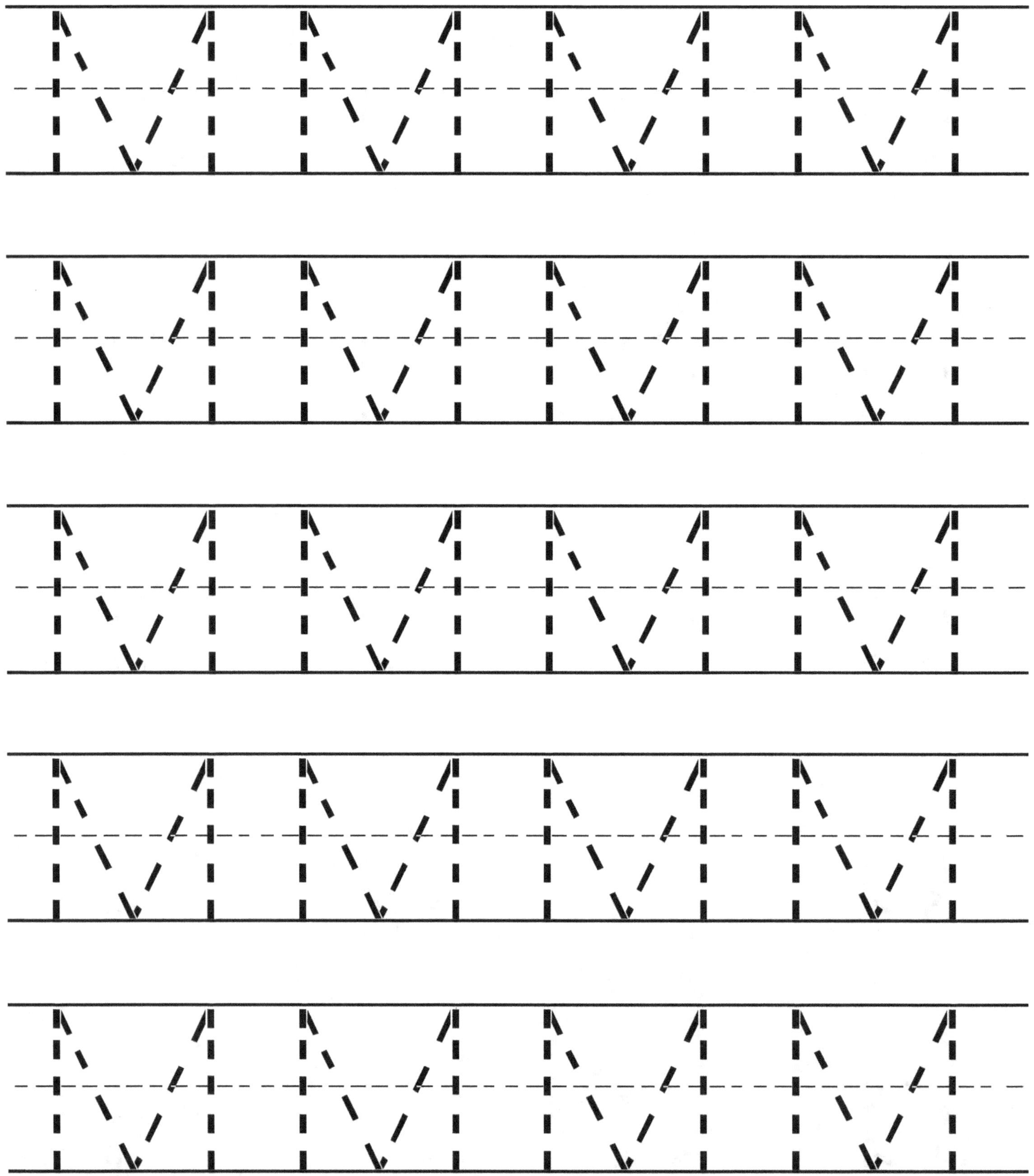

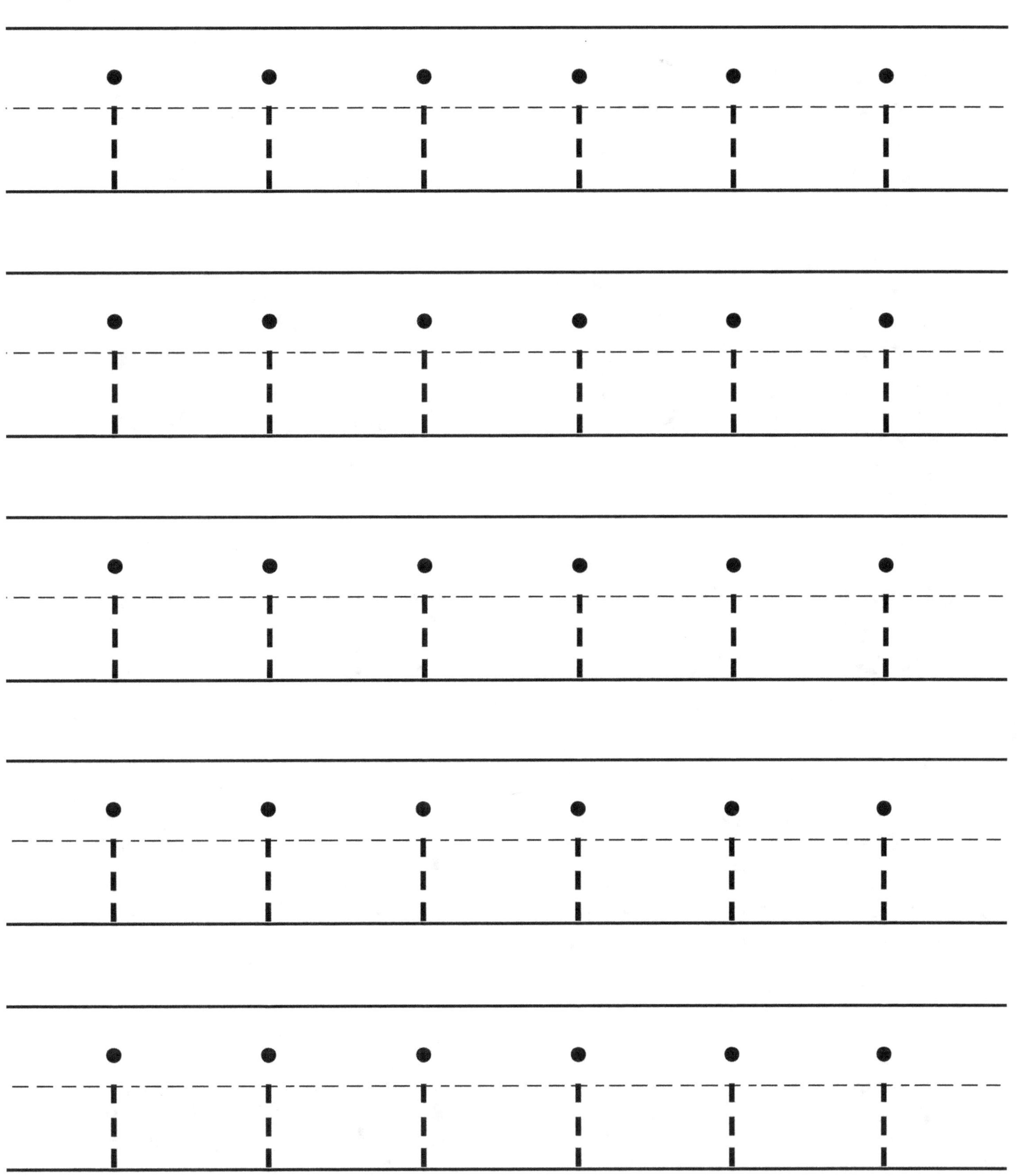

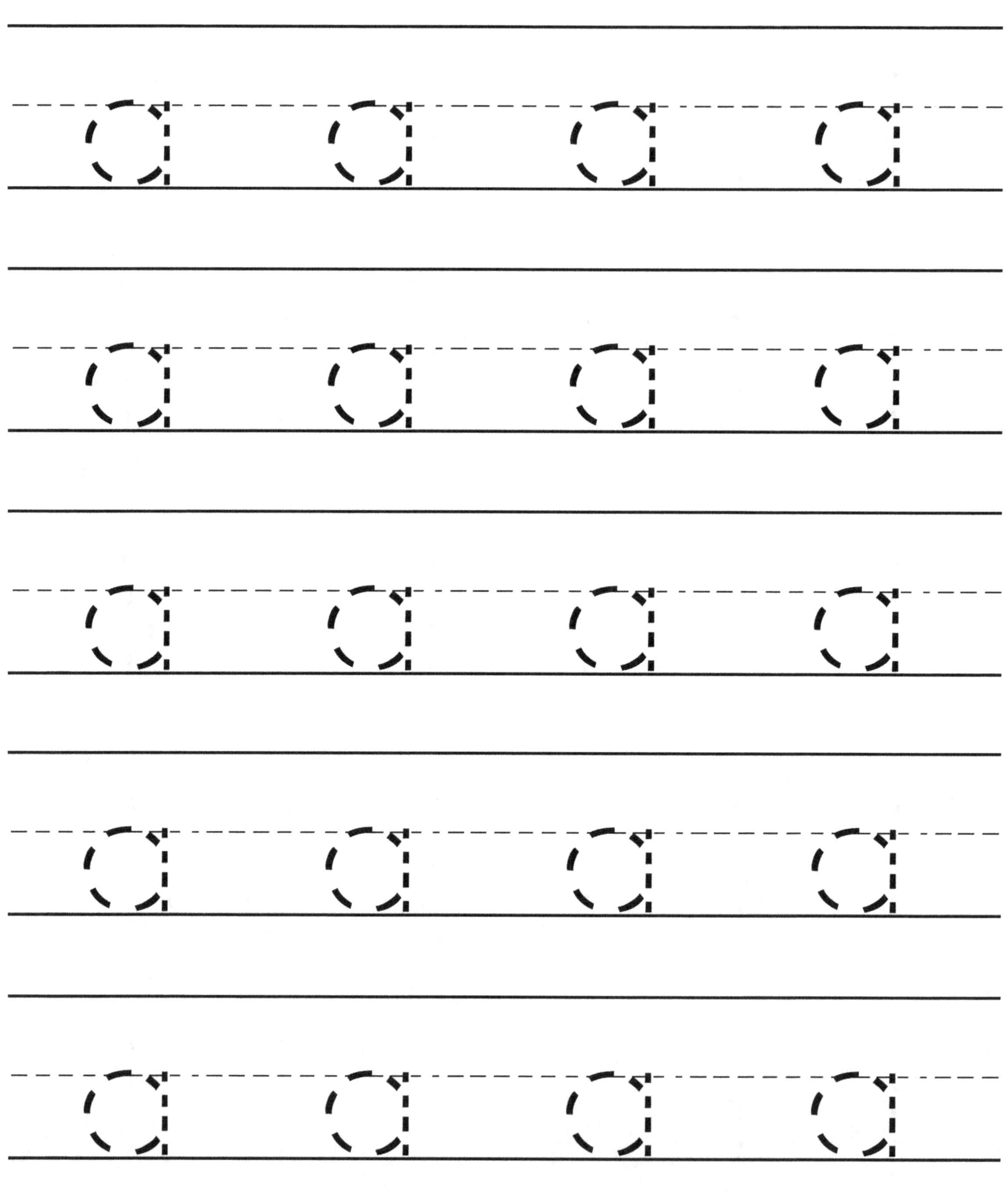

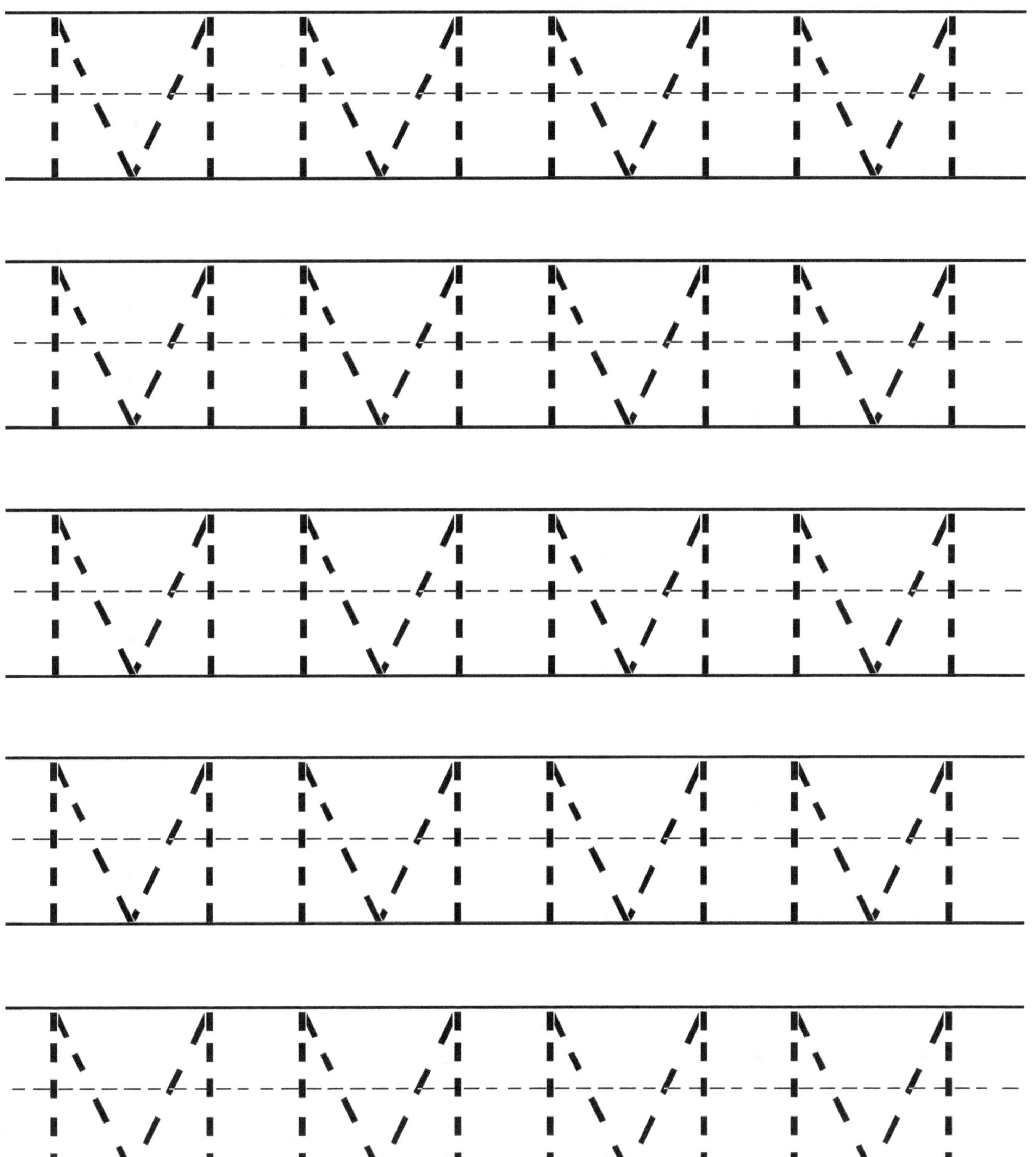

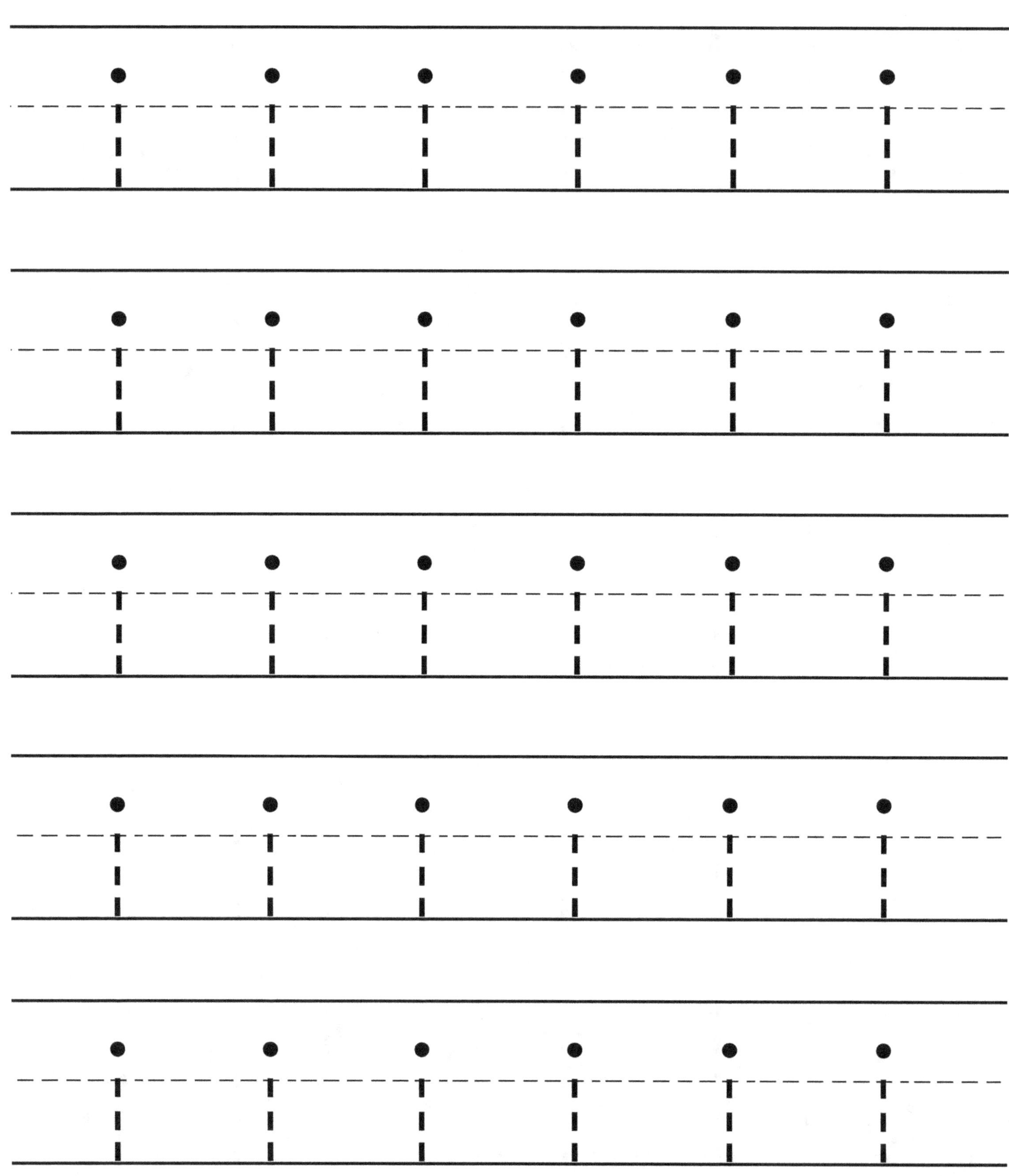

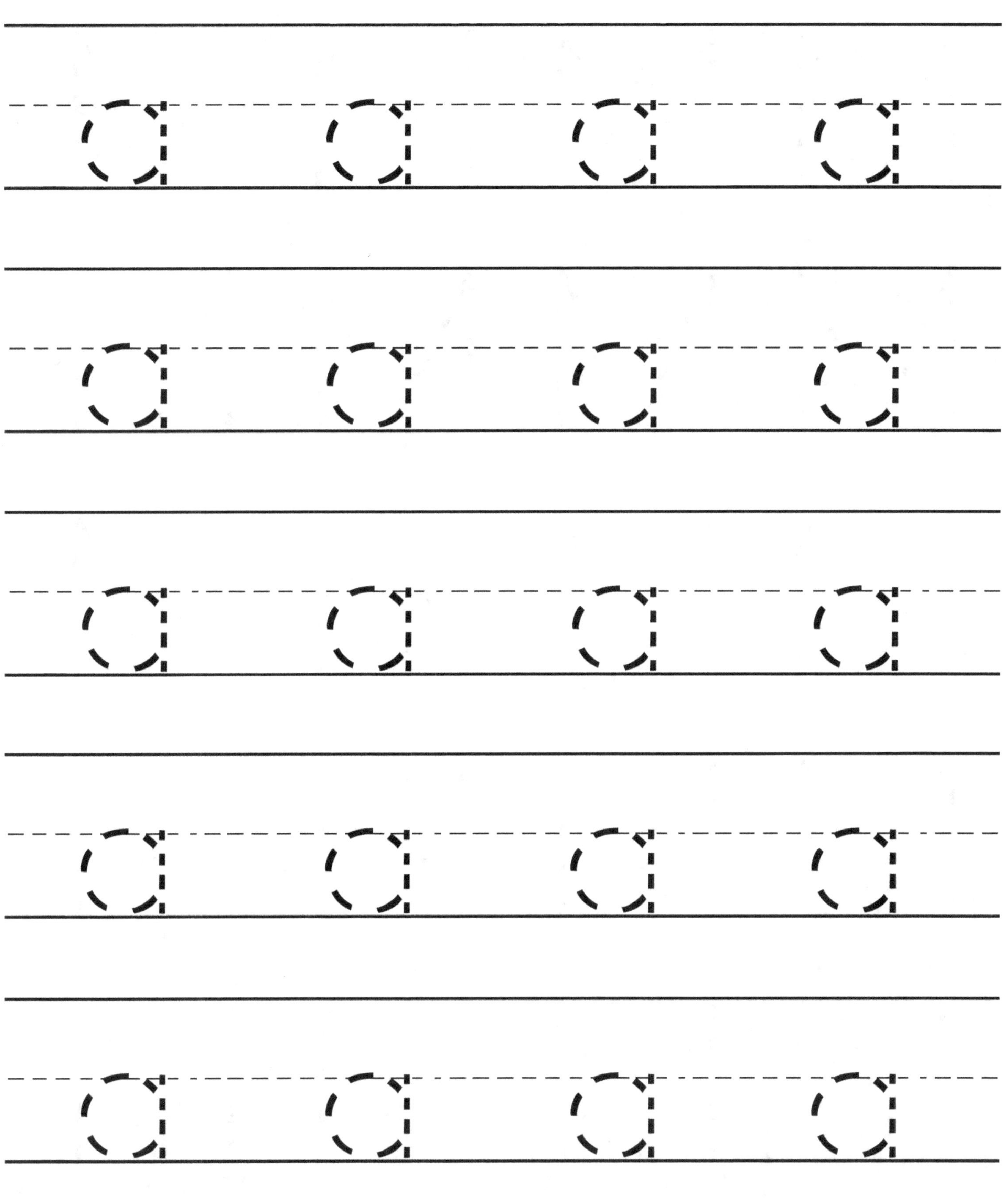

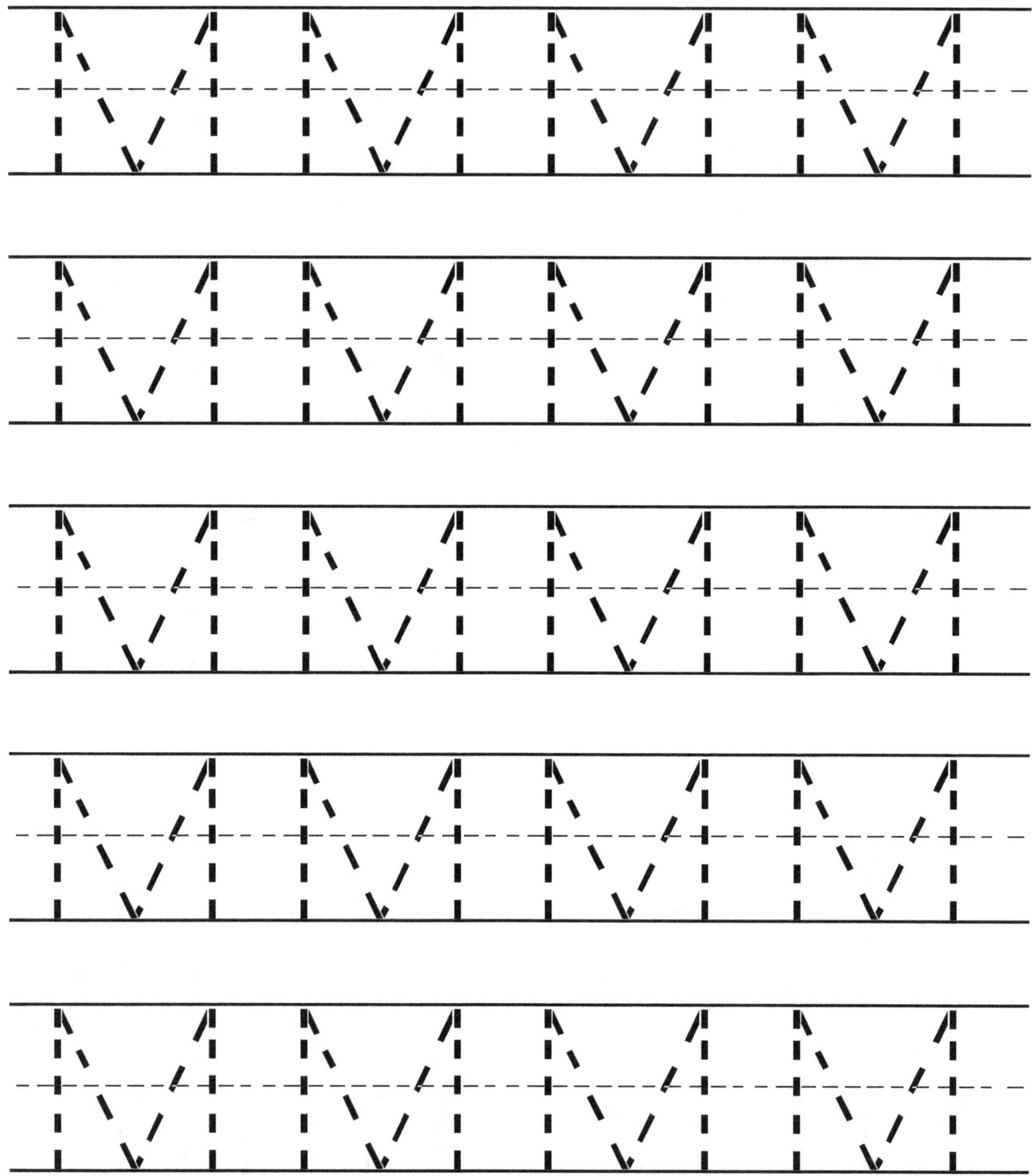

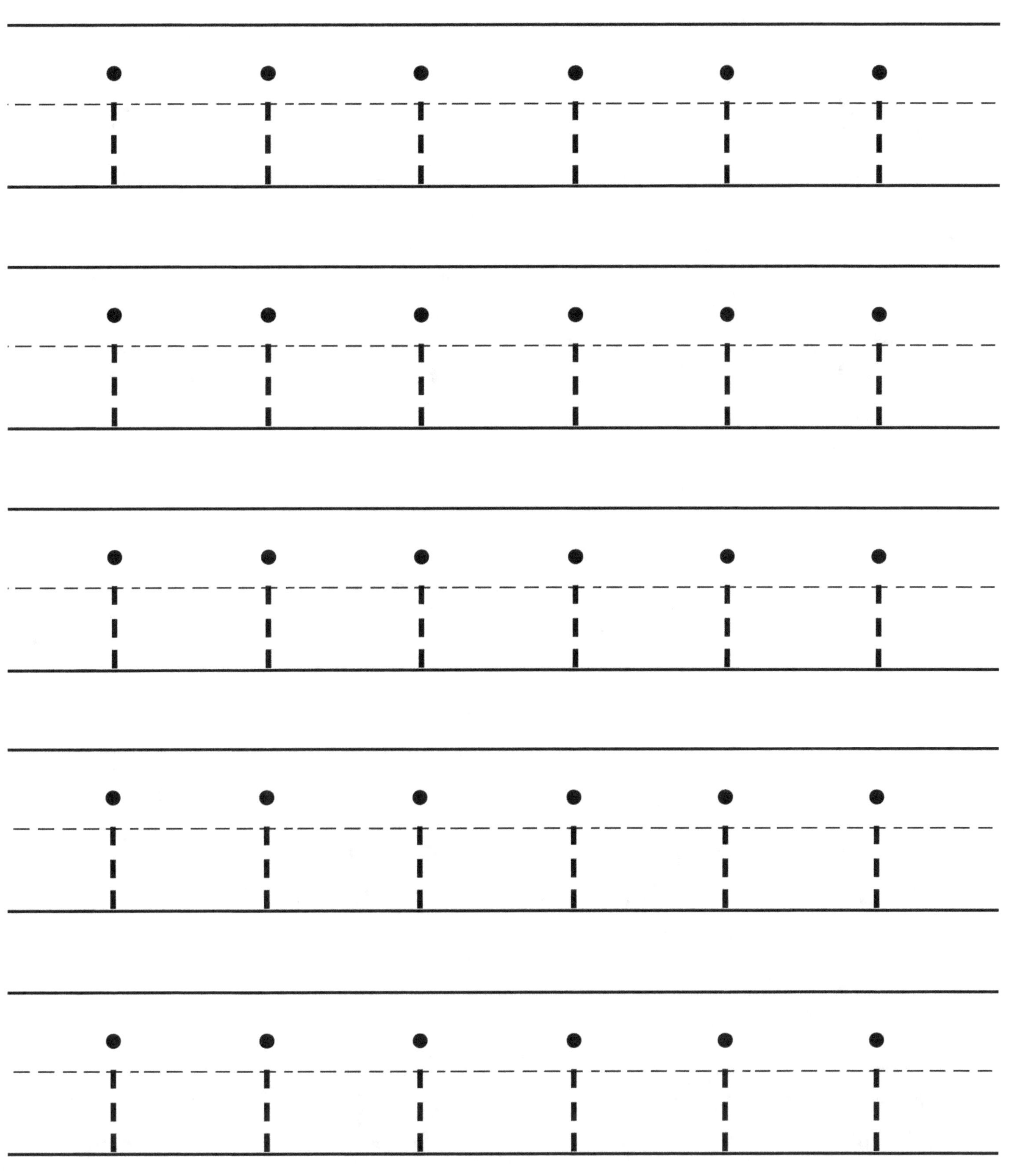

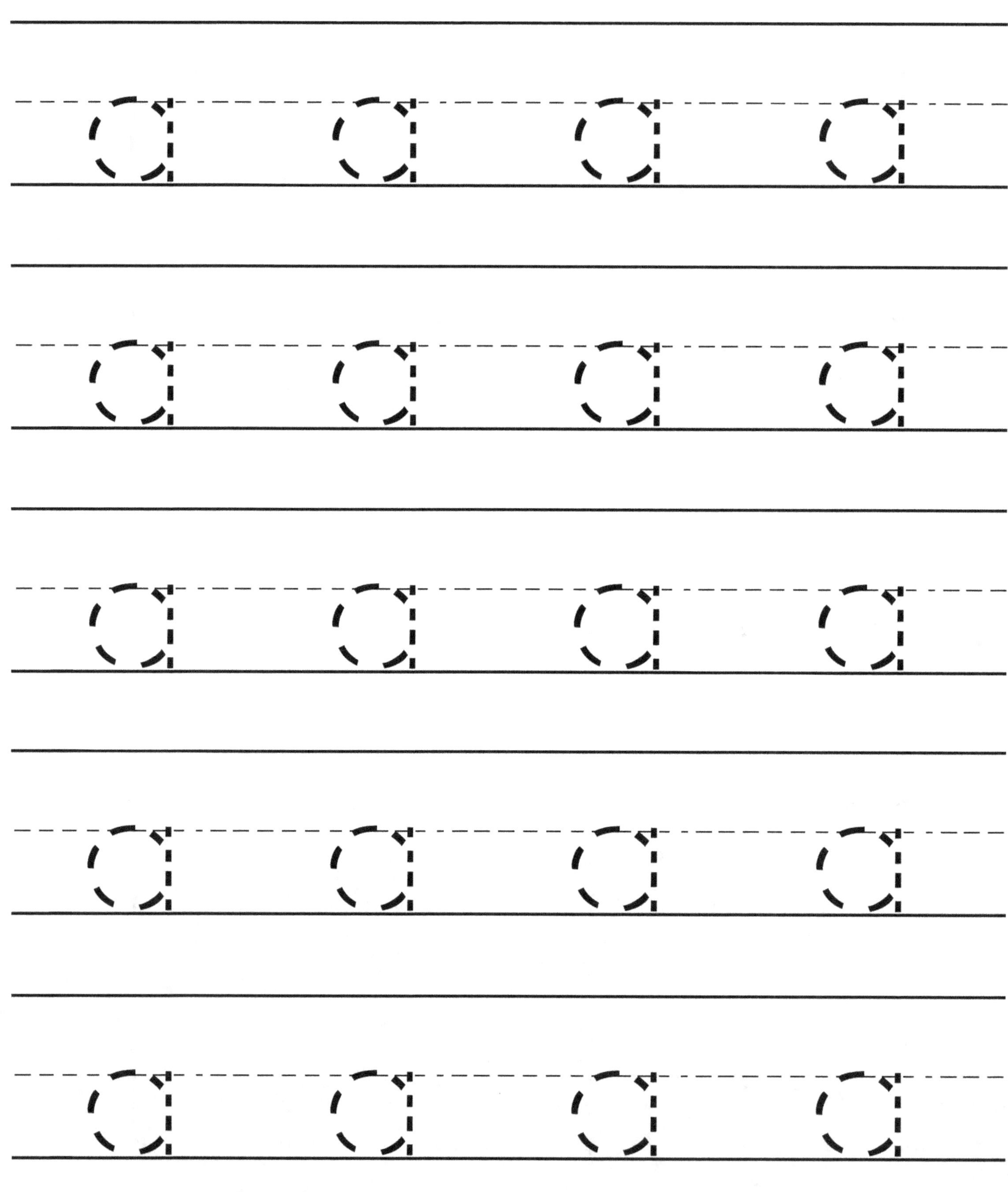

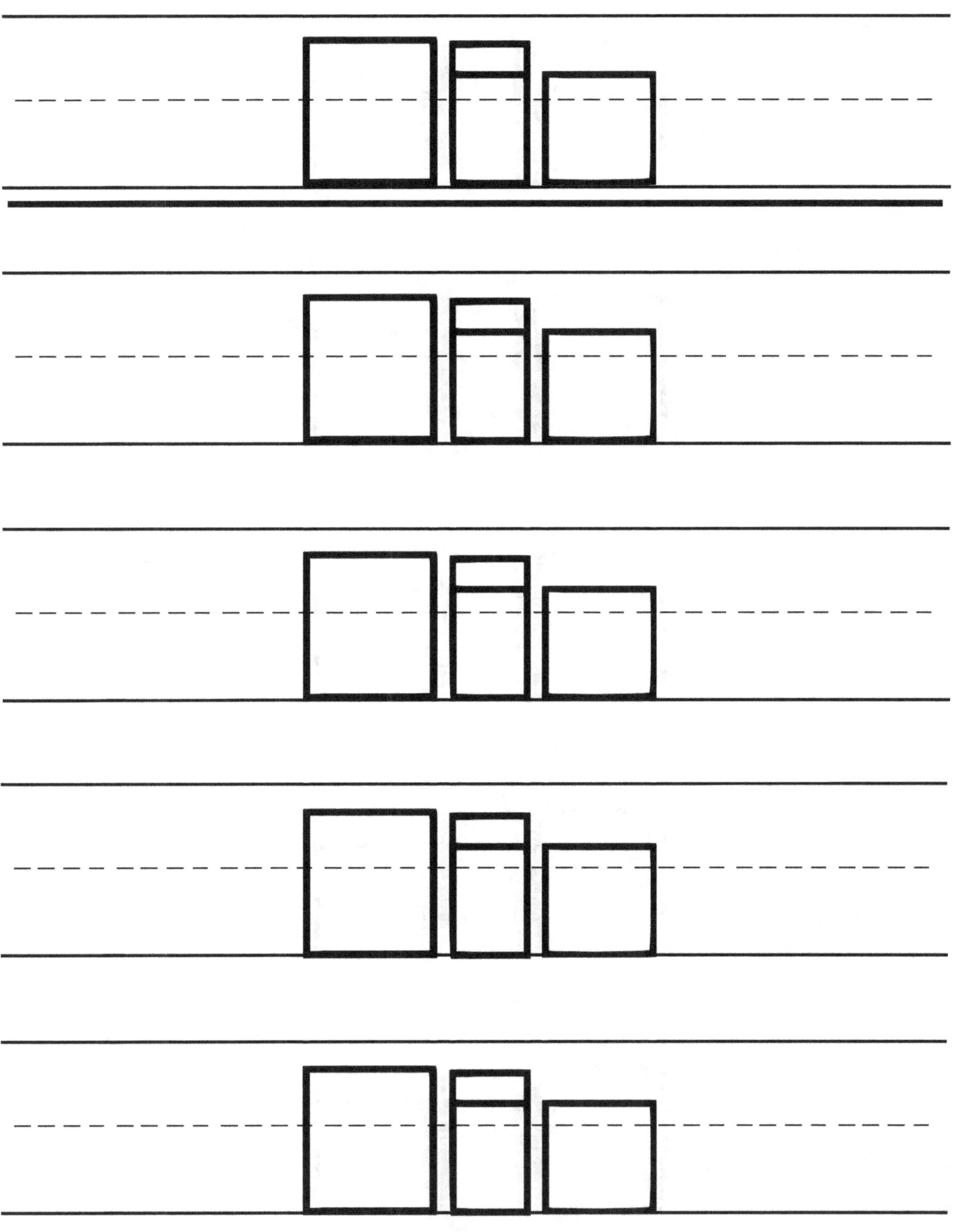

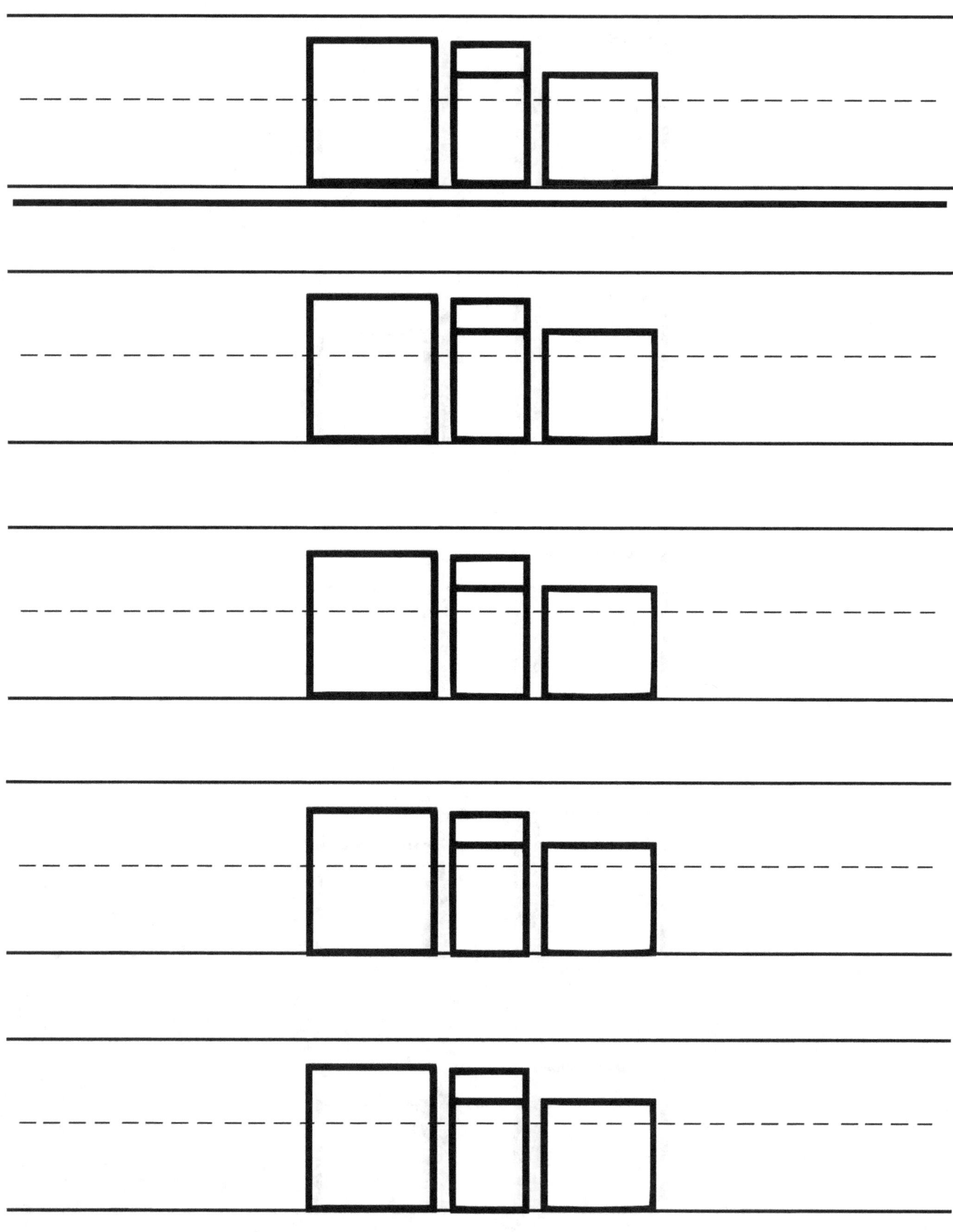

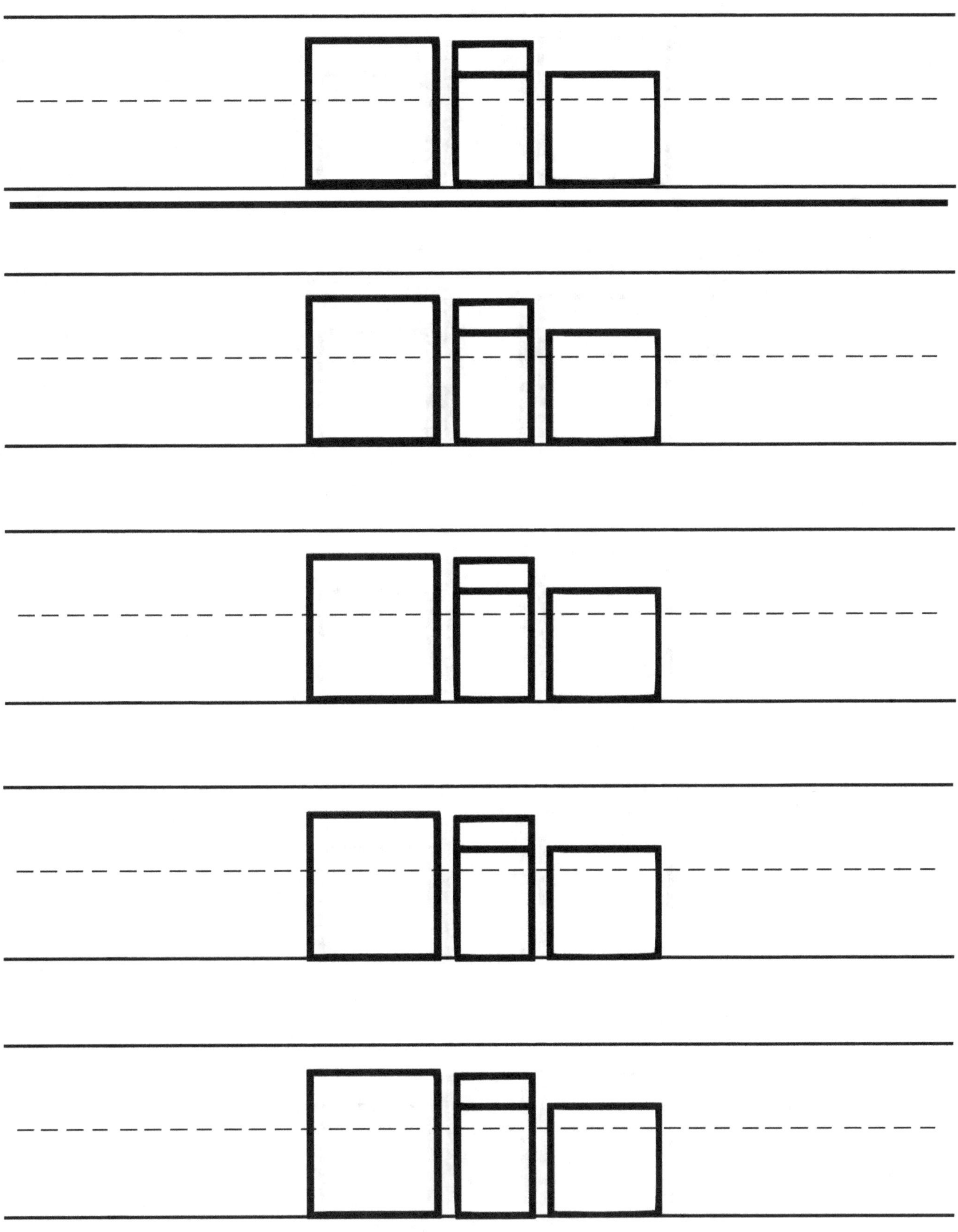

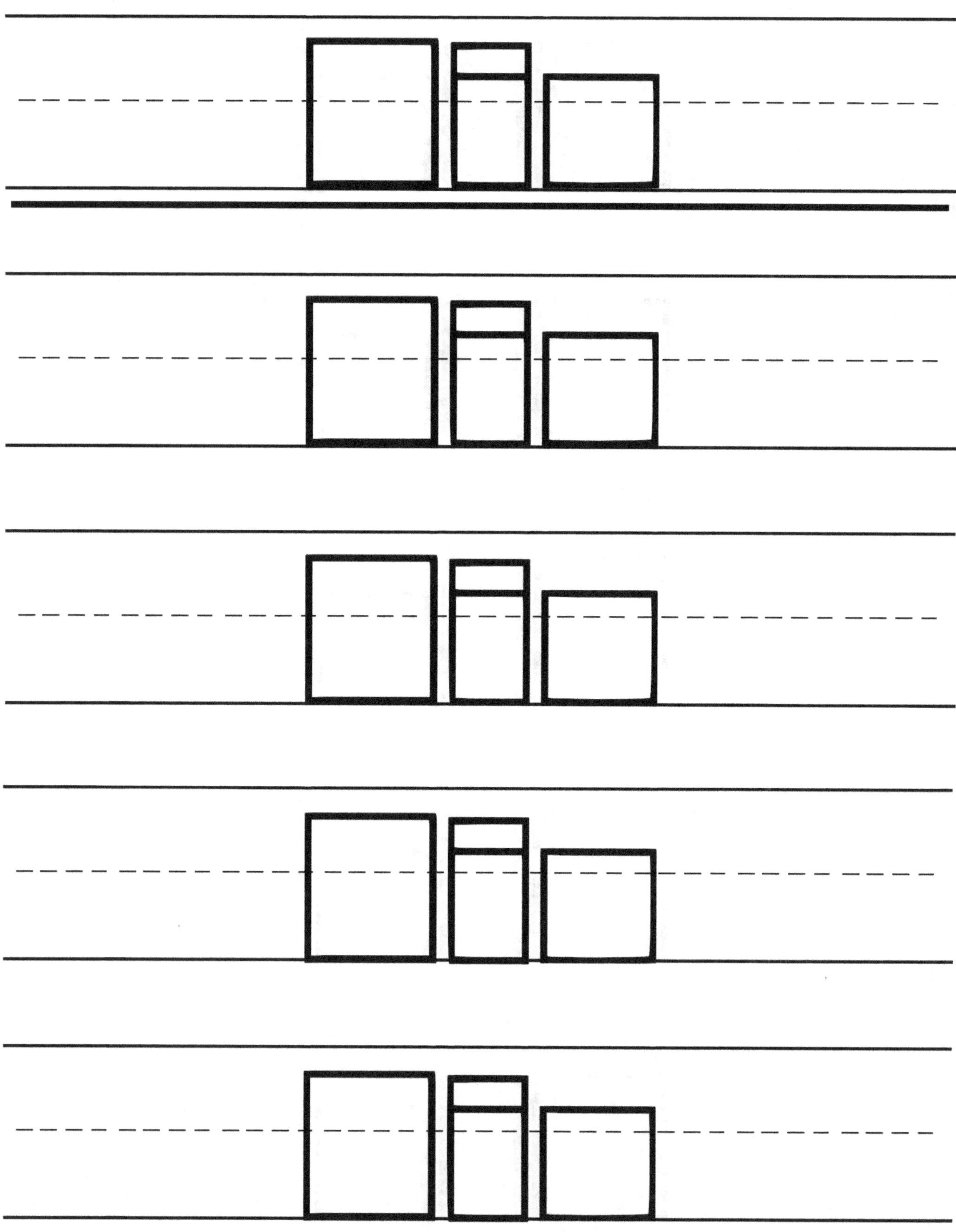

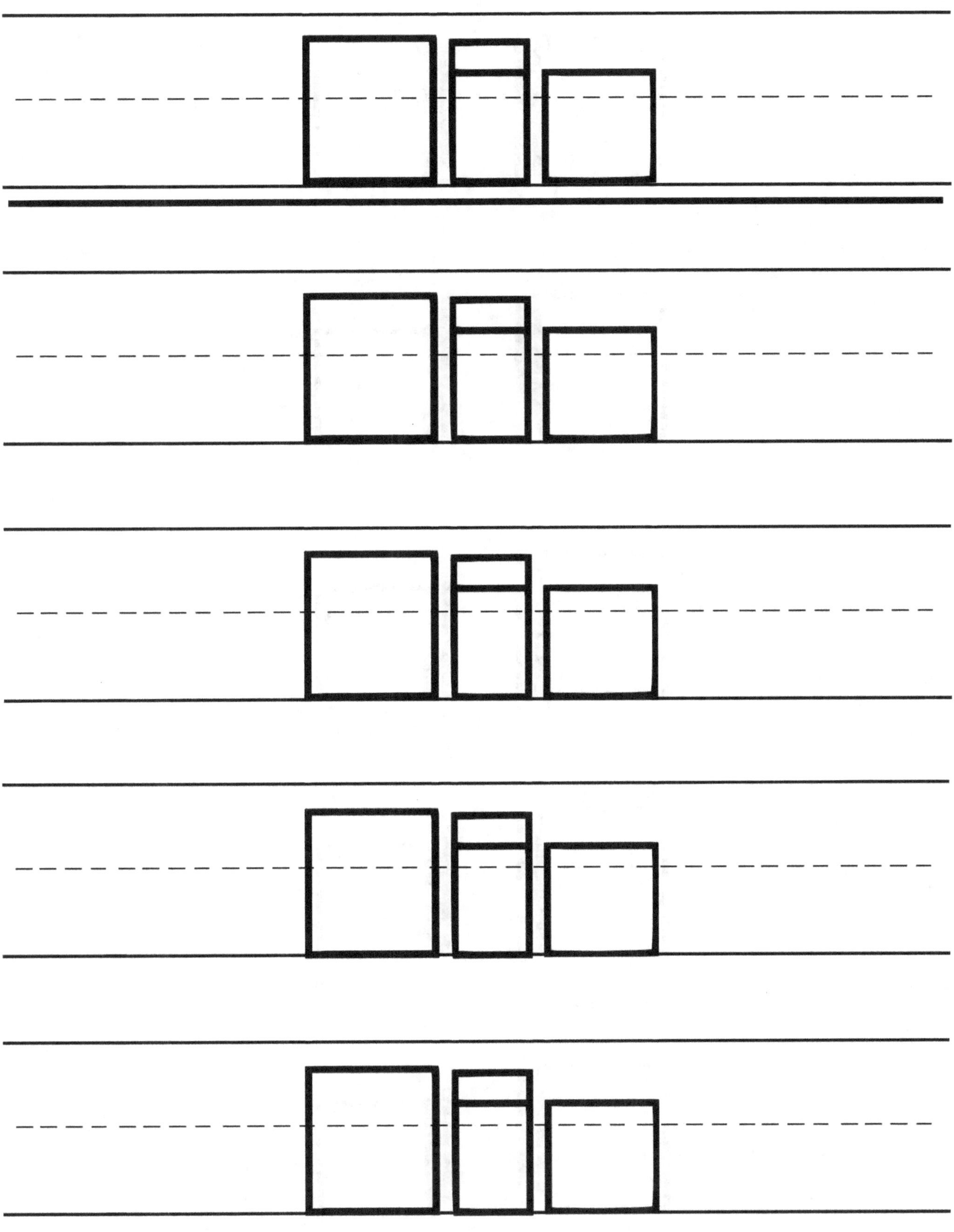

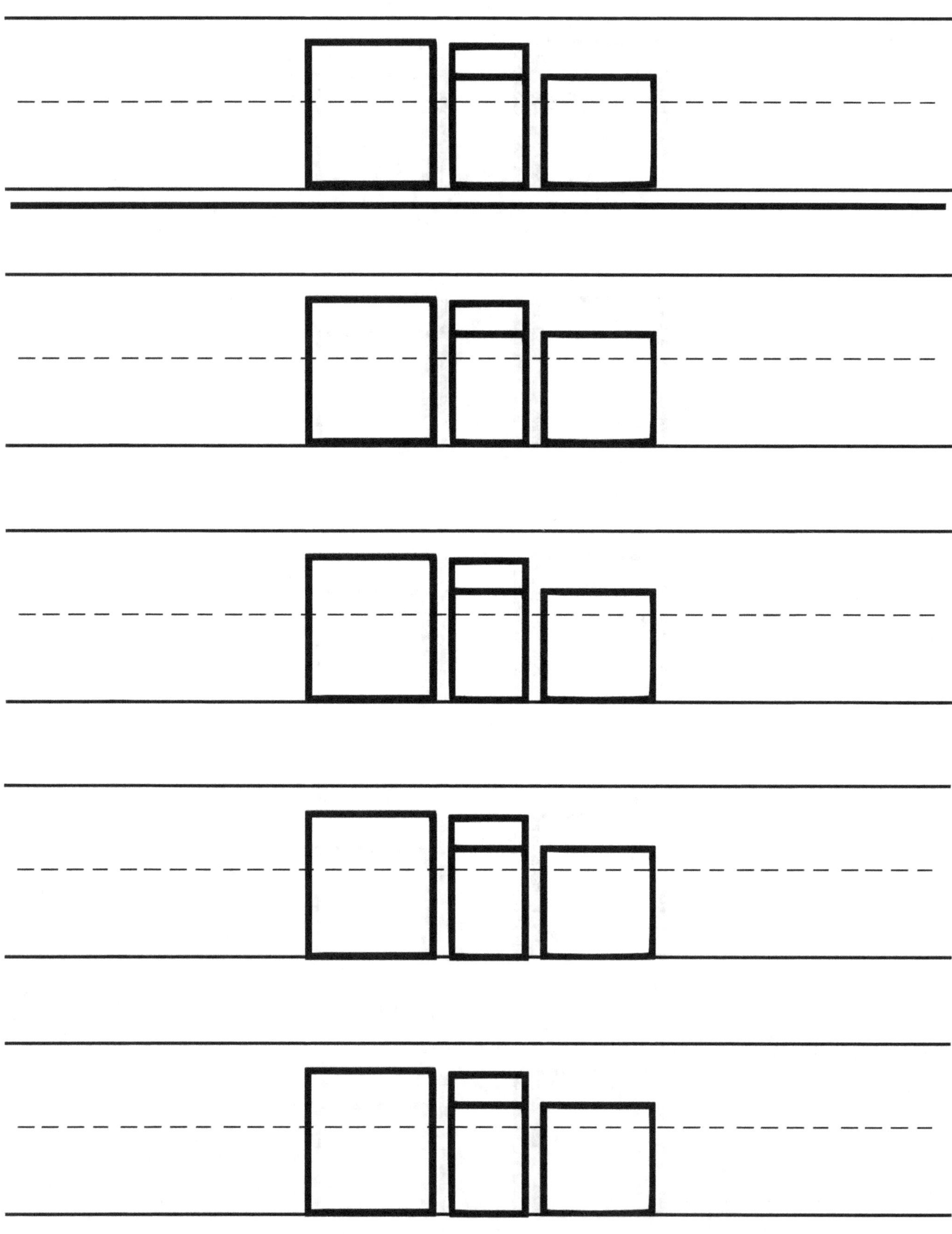

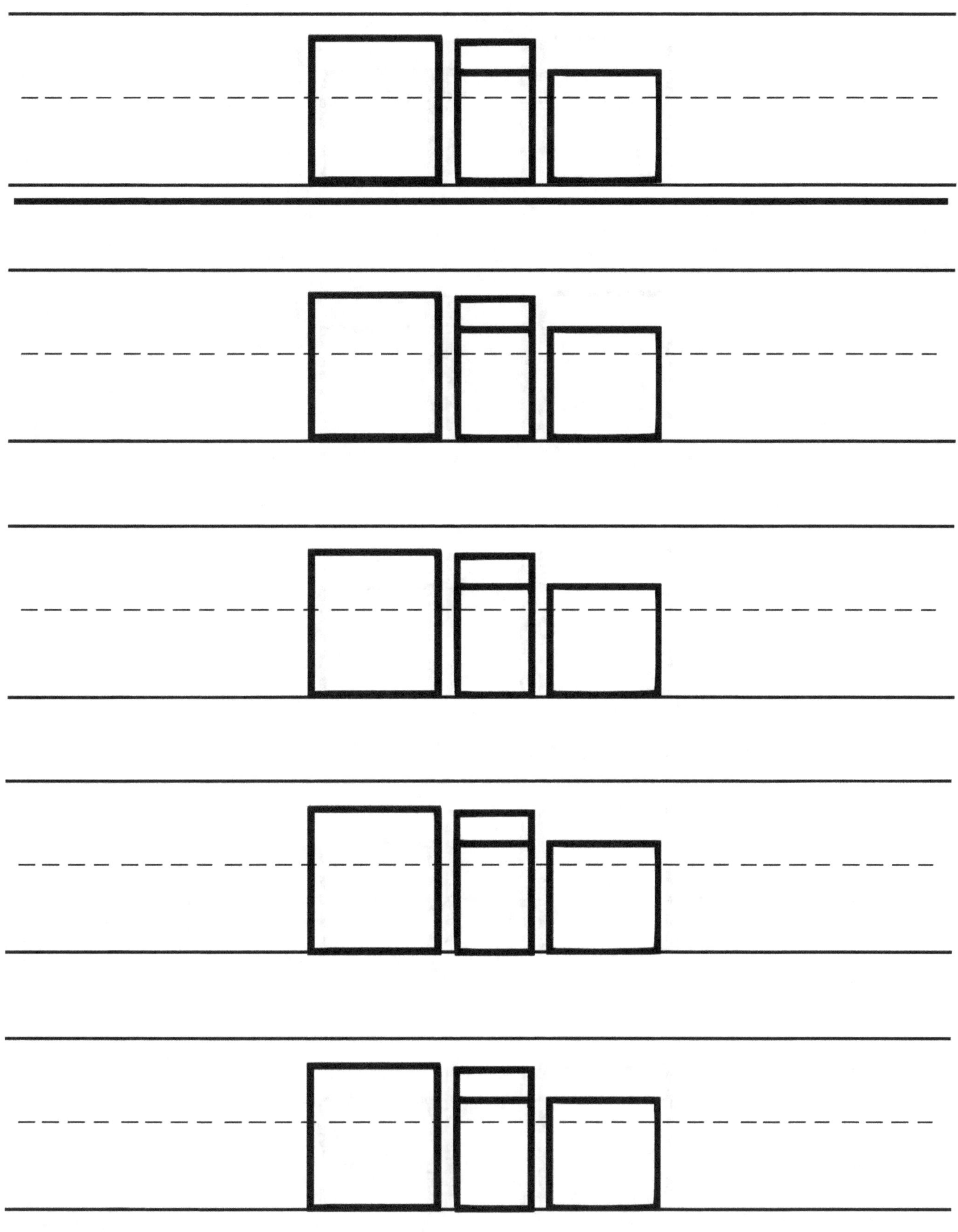

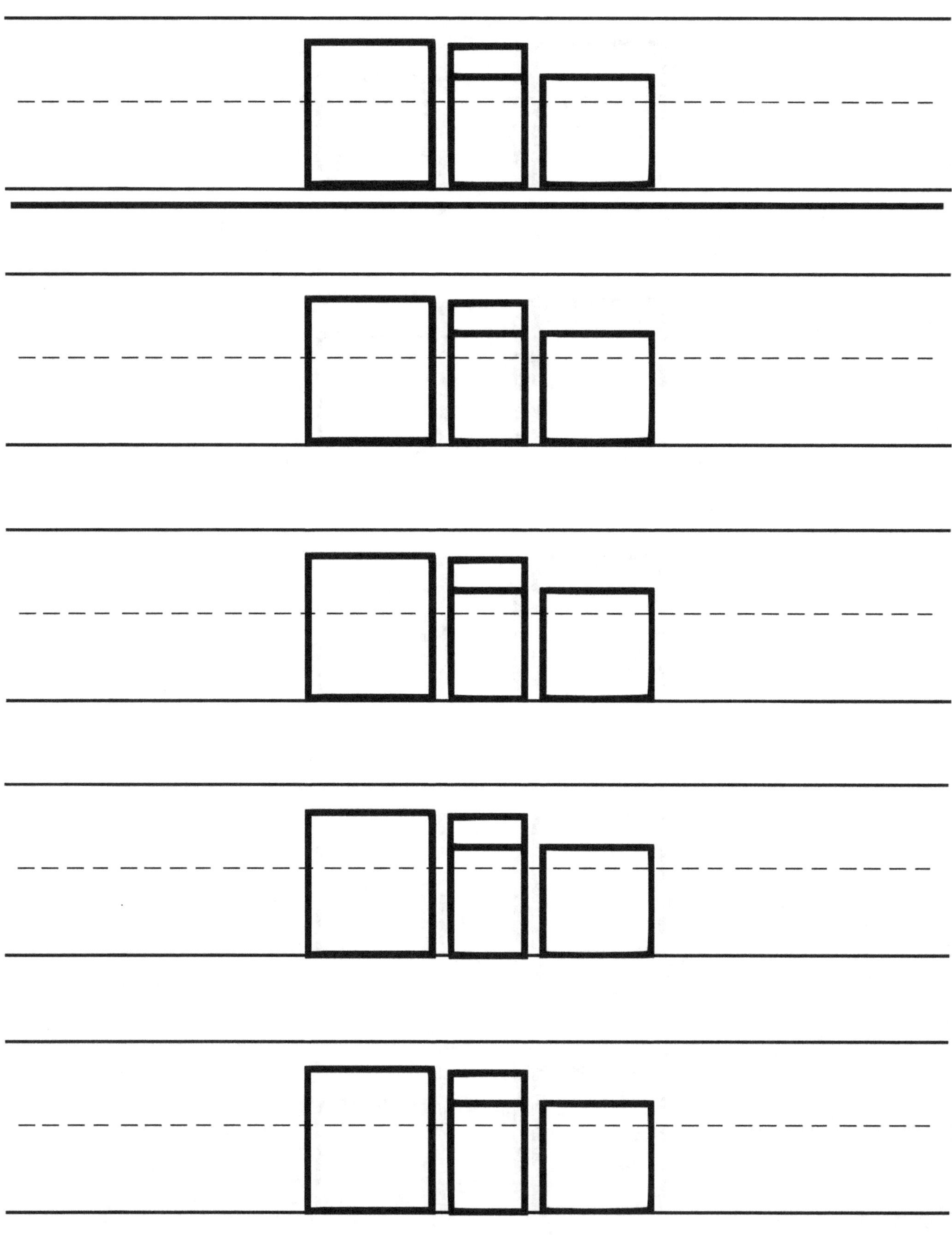

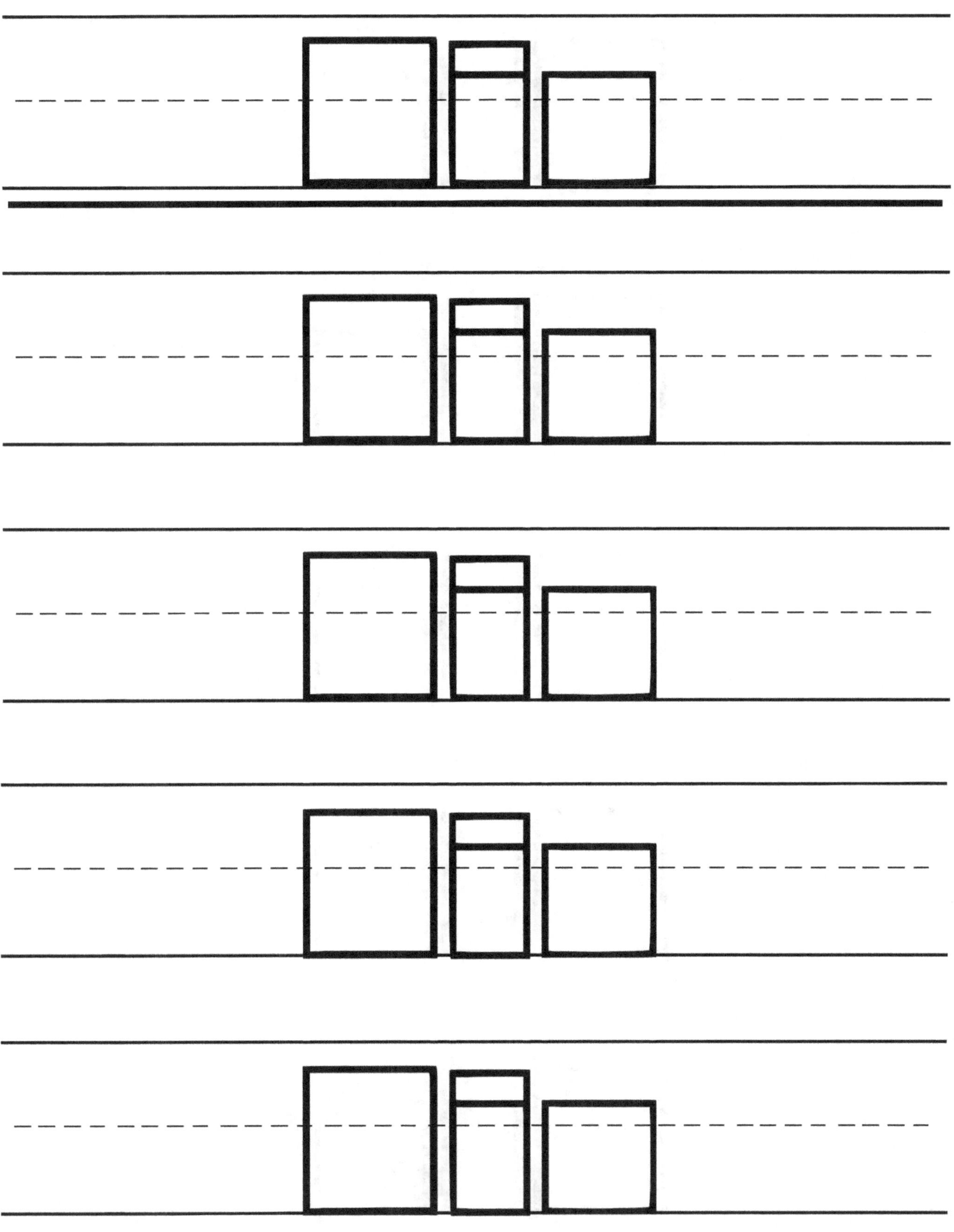

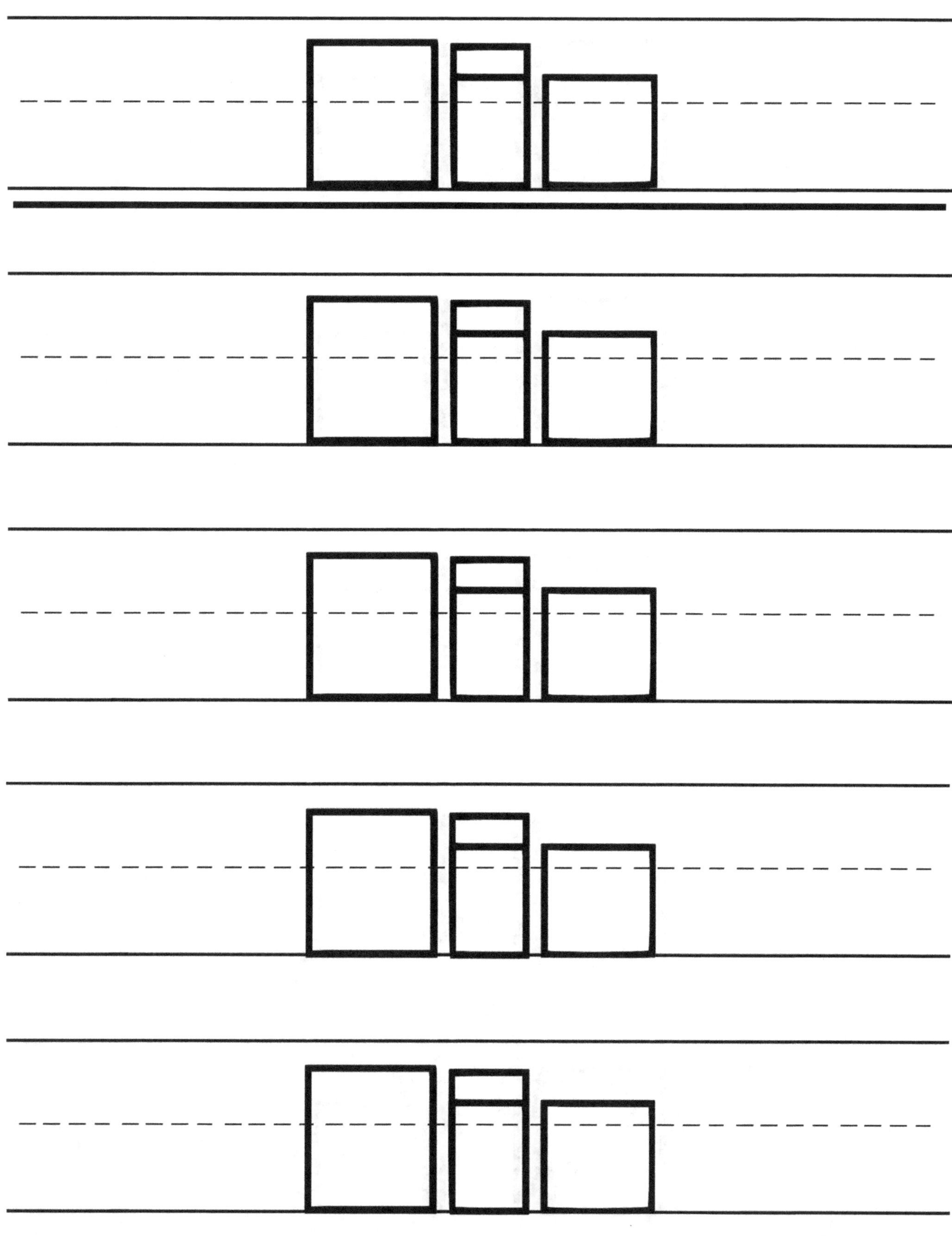

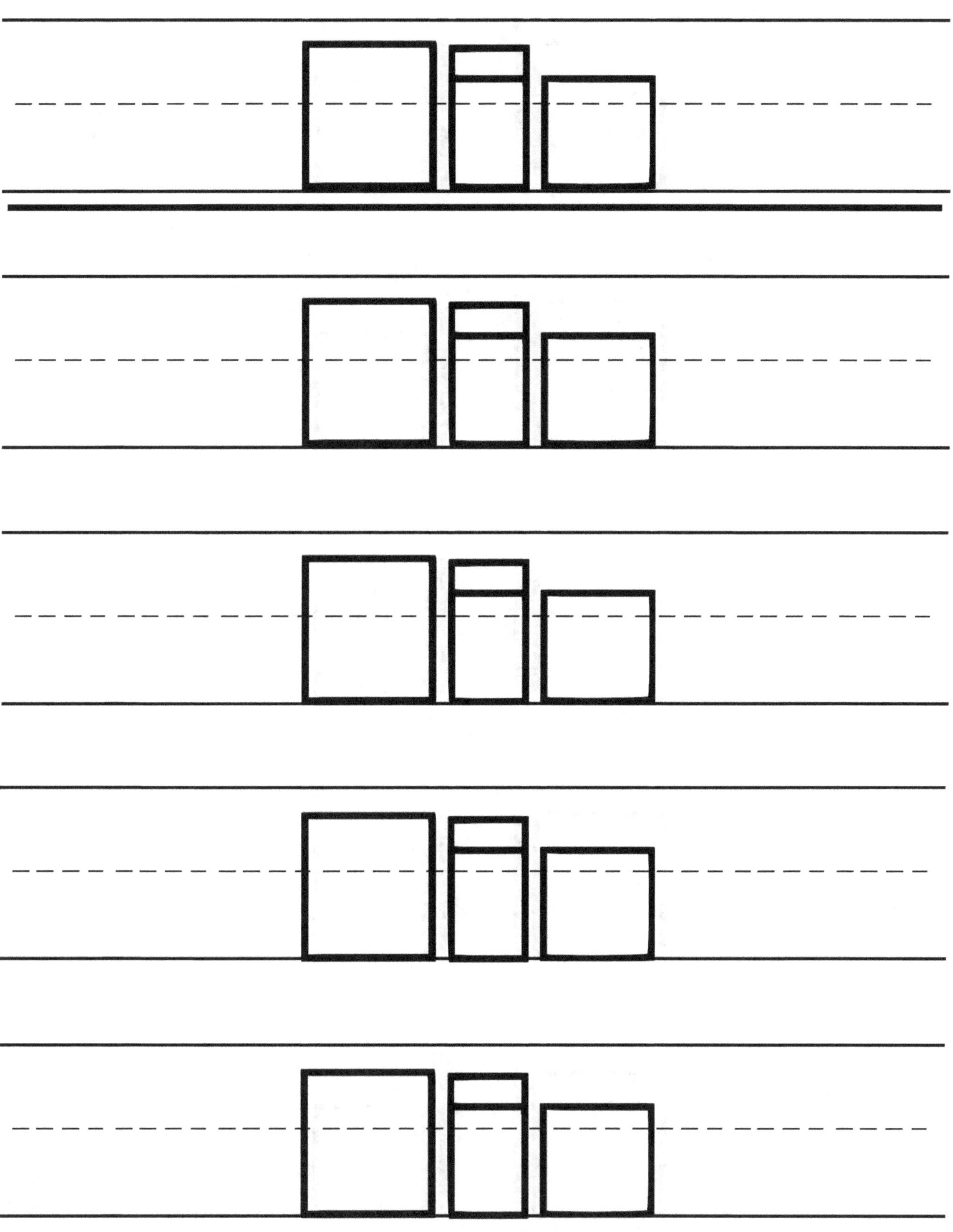

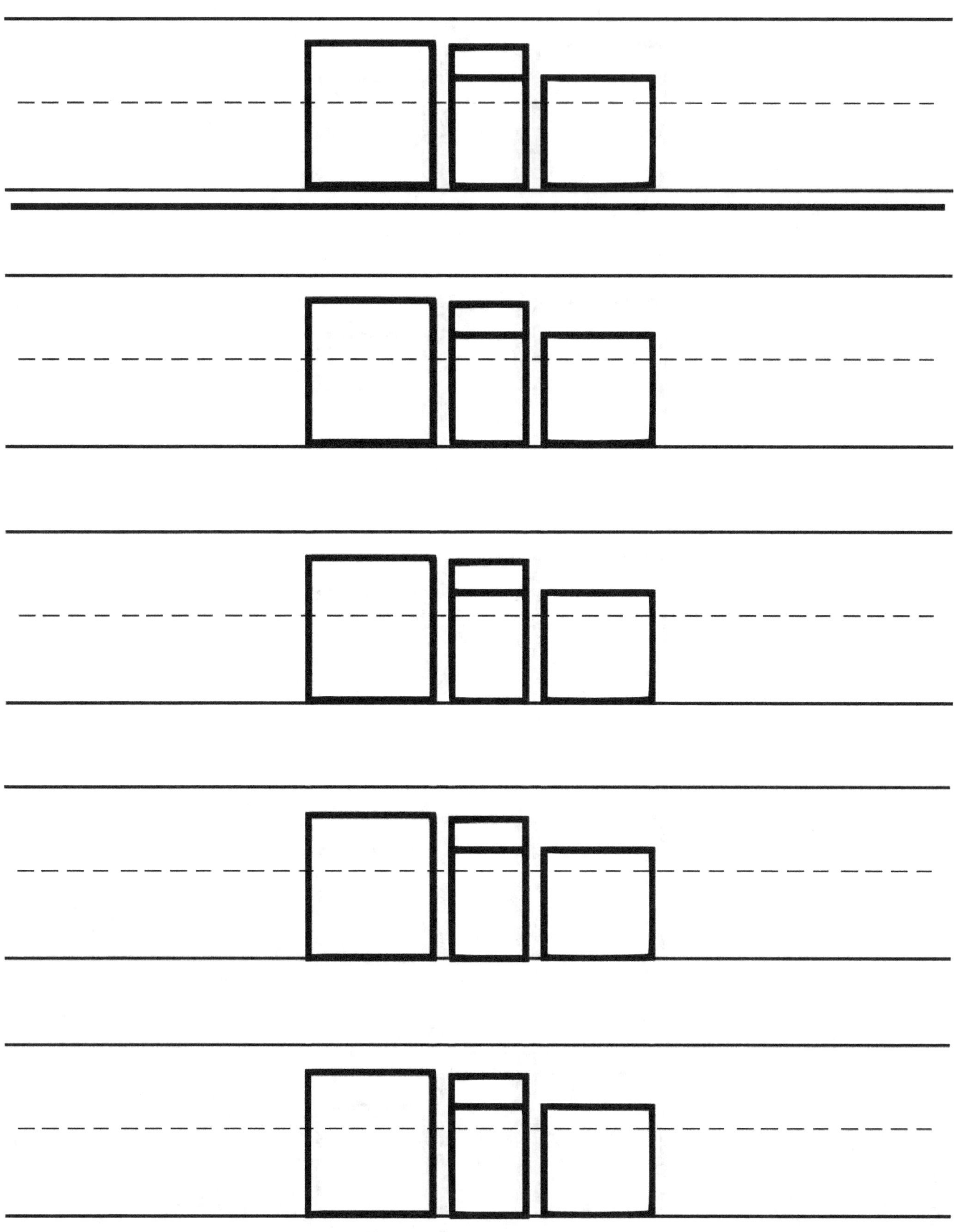

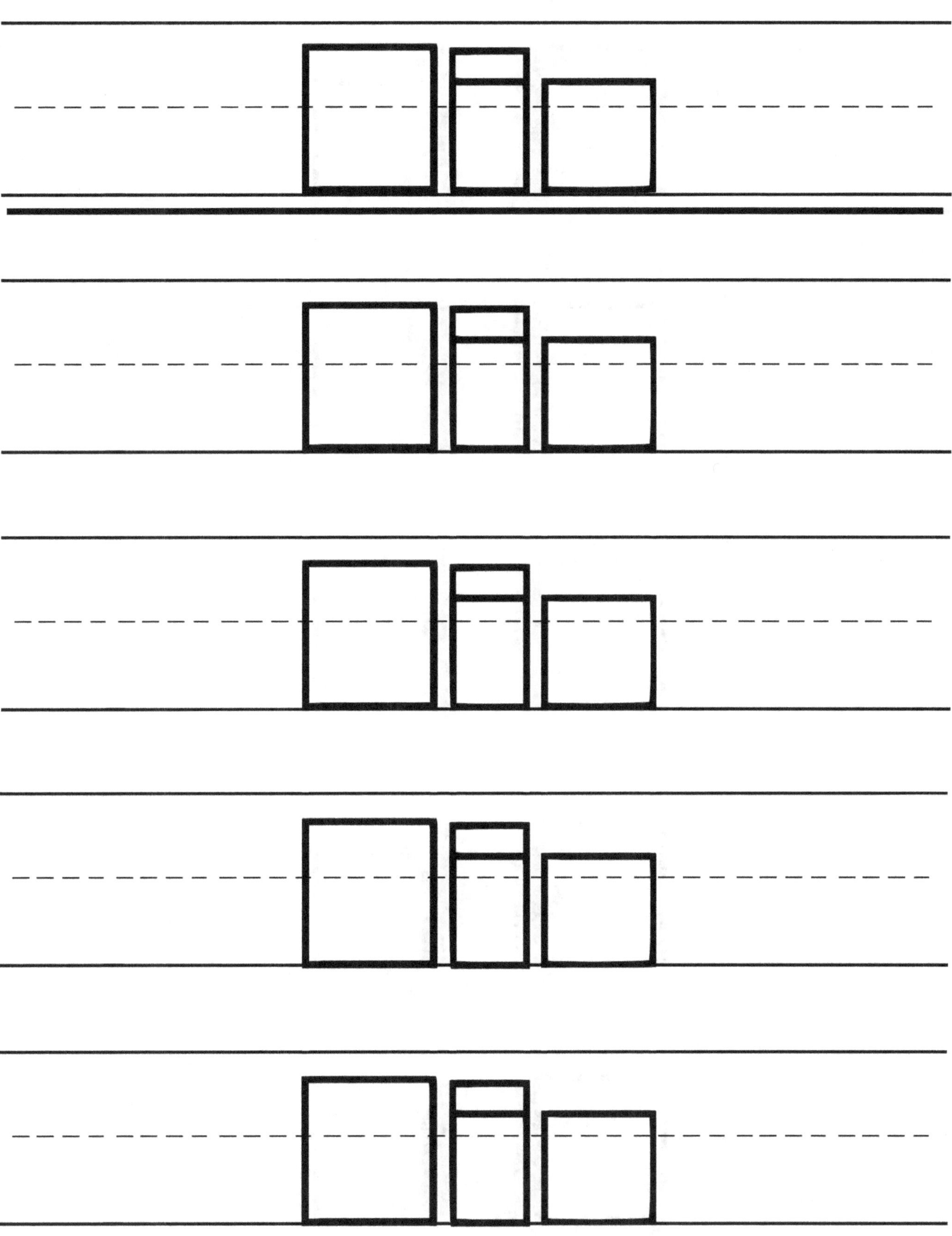

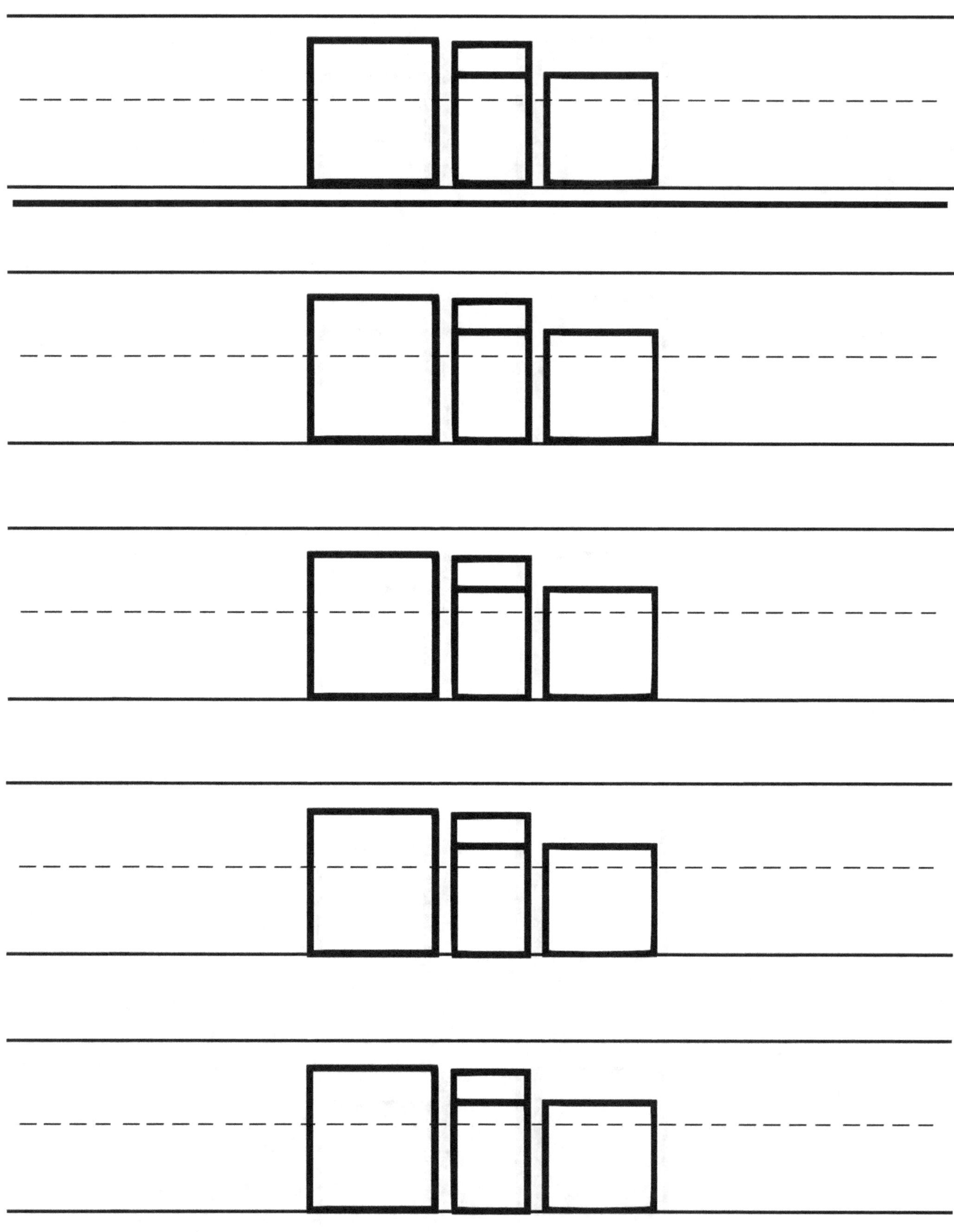

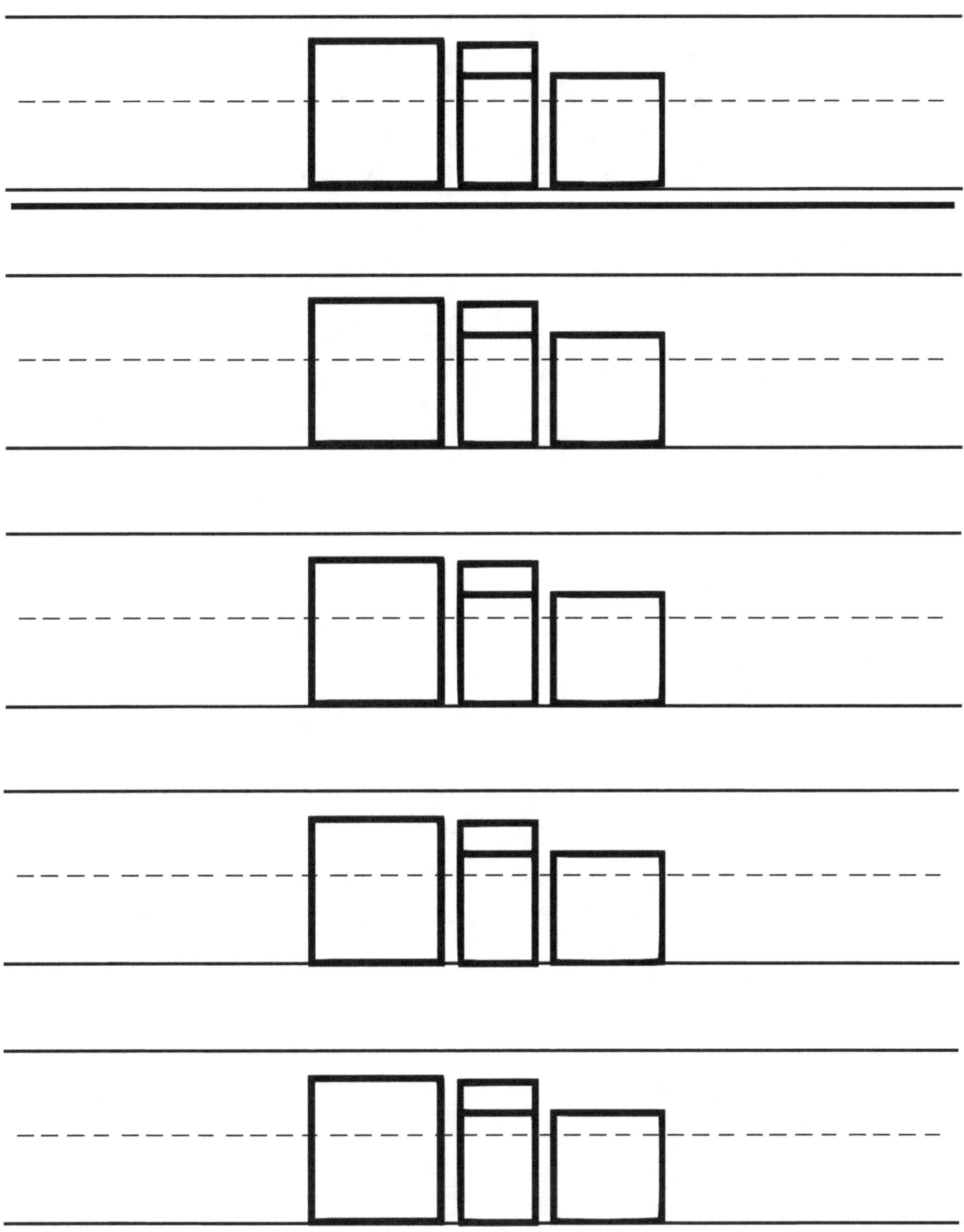

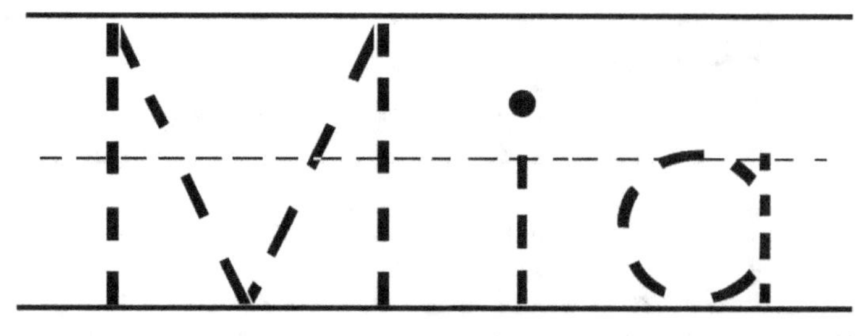

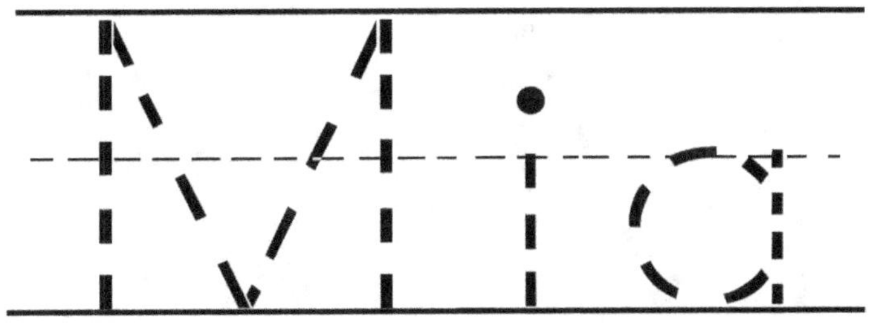

Mia

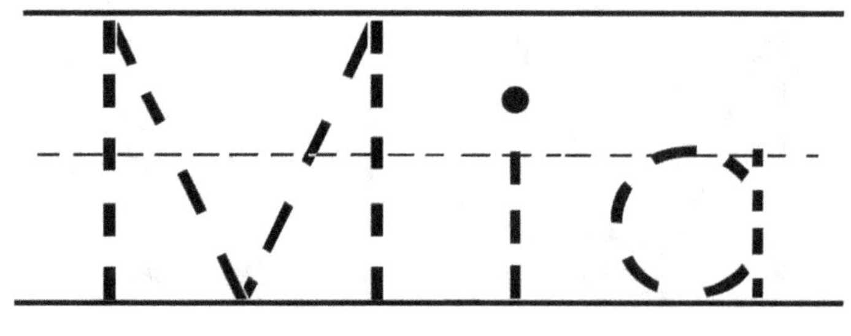

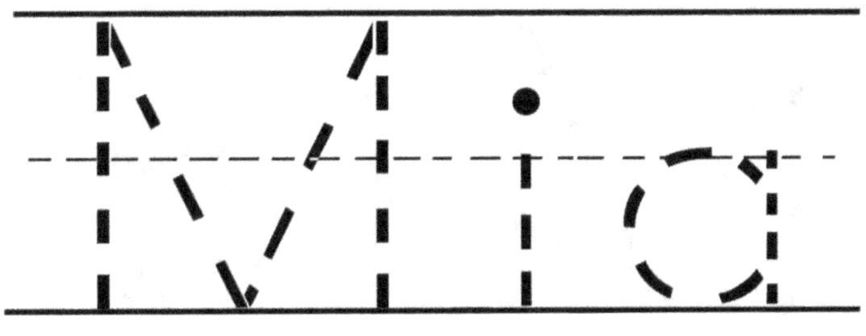

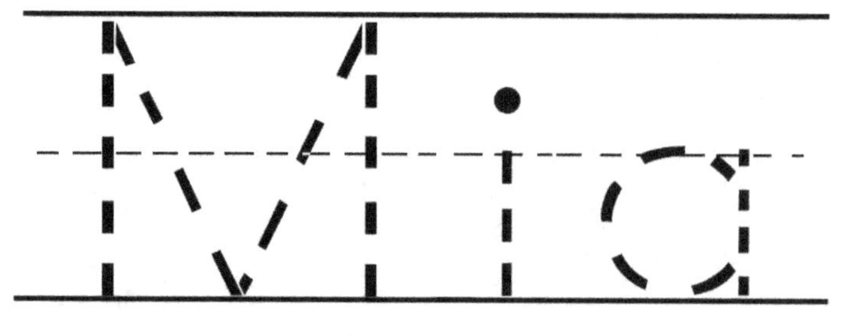

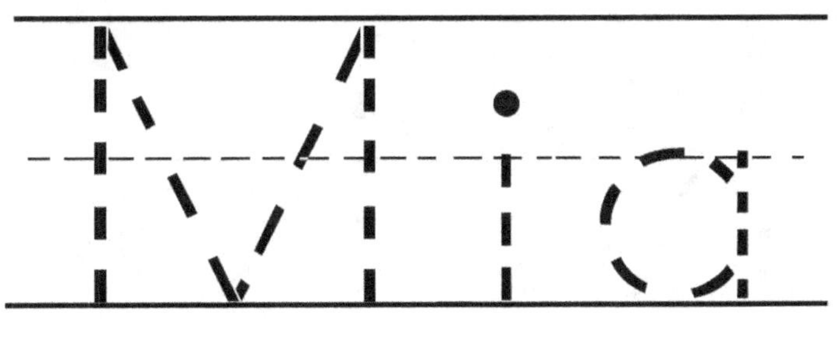

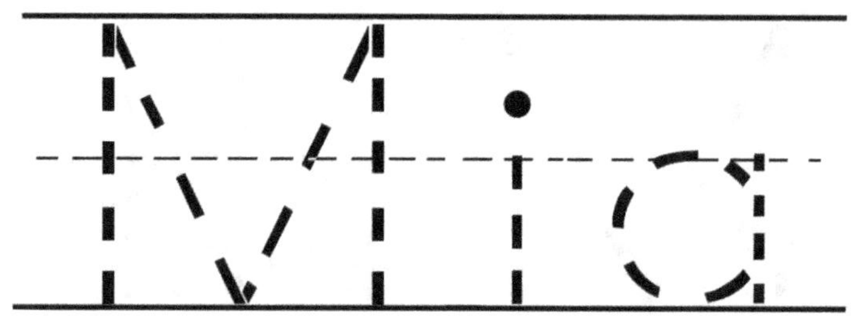

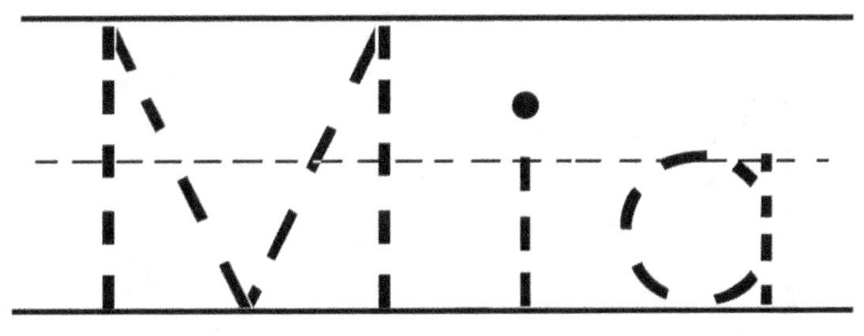

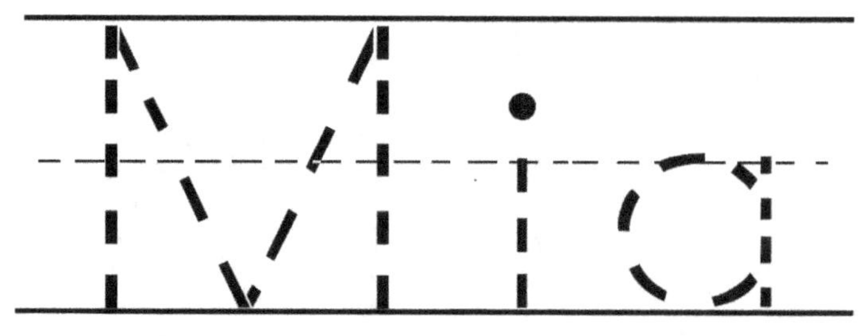

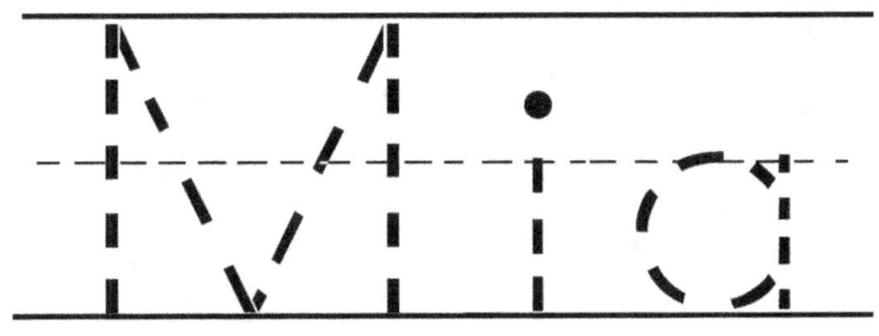

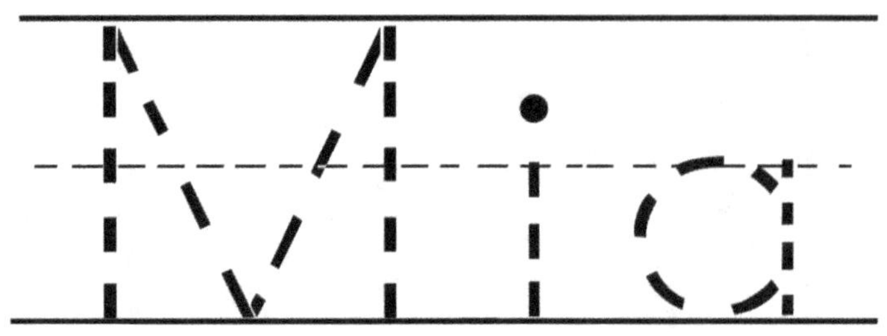

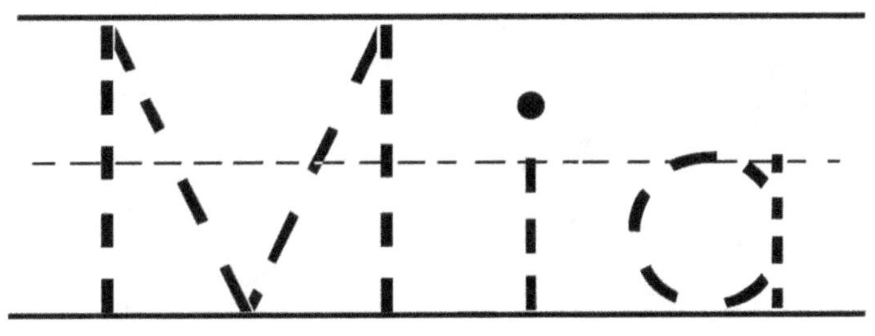

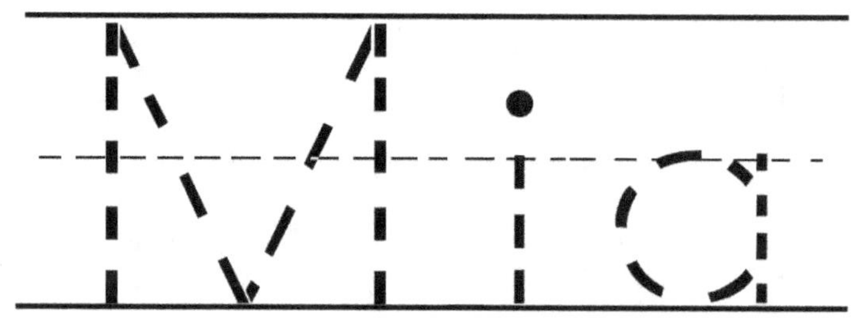

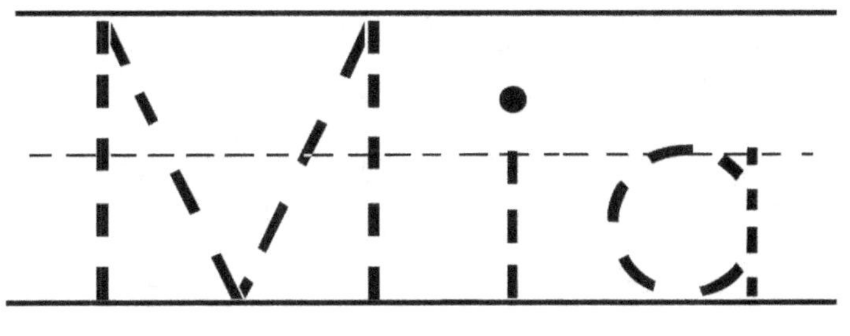

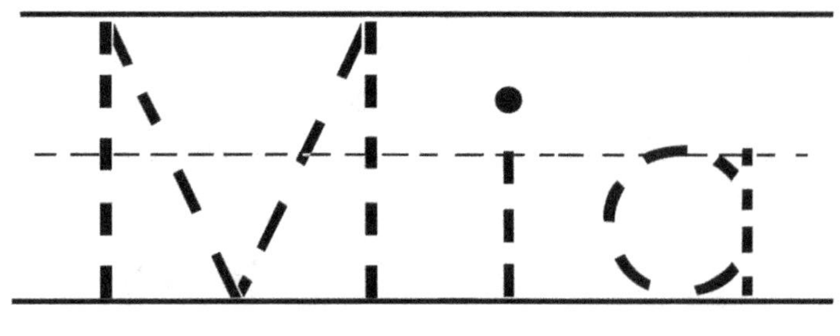
Mia

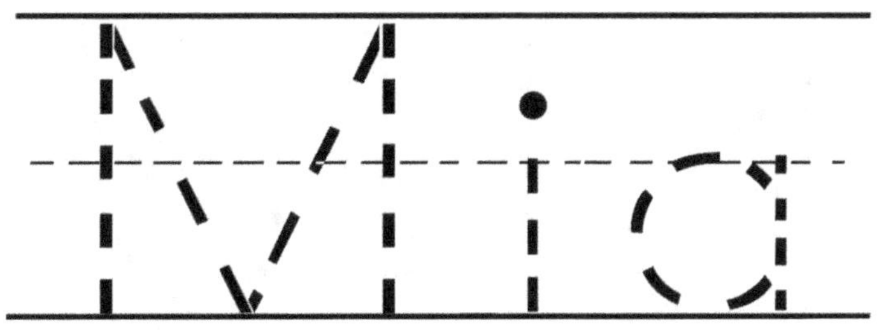
Mia

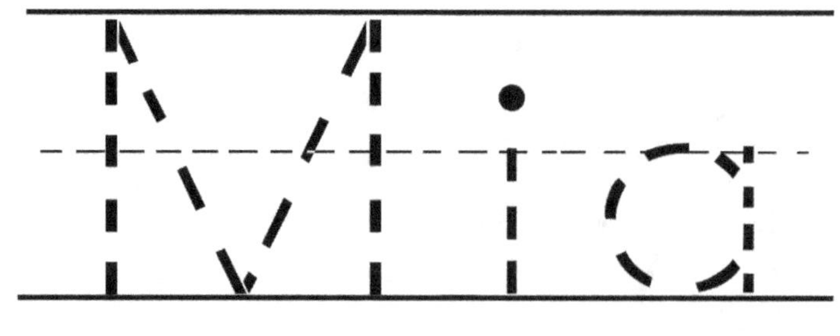
Mia

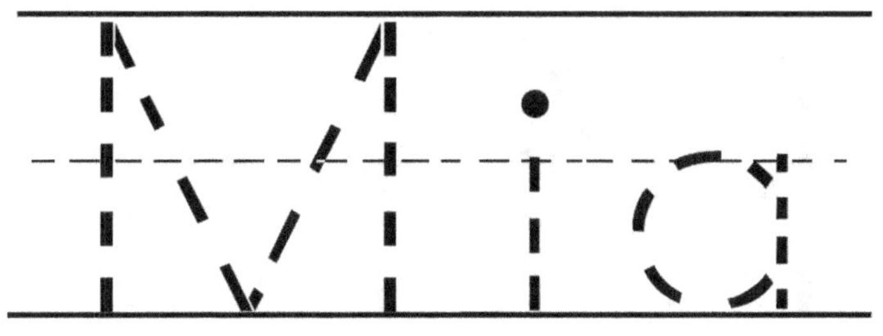

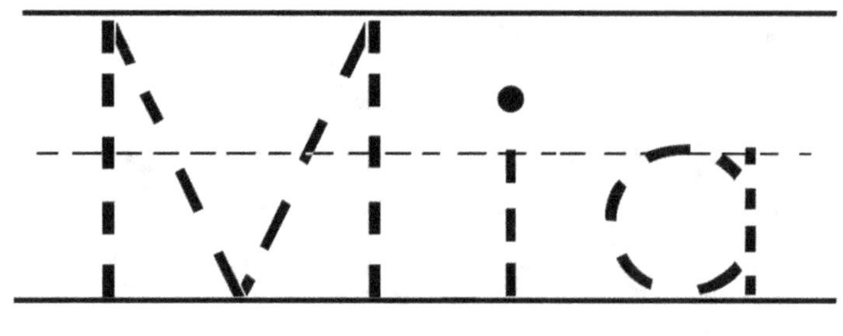

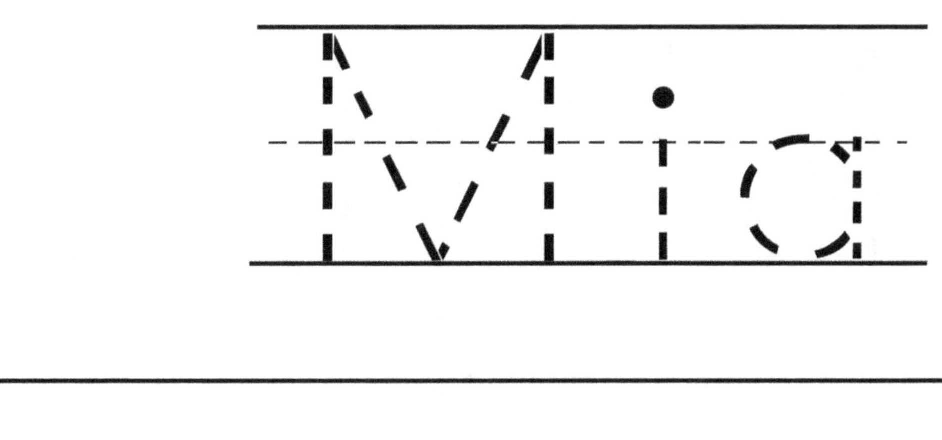

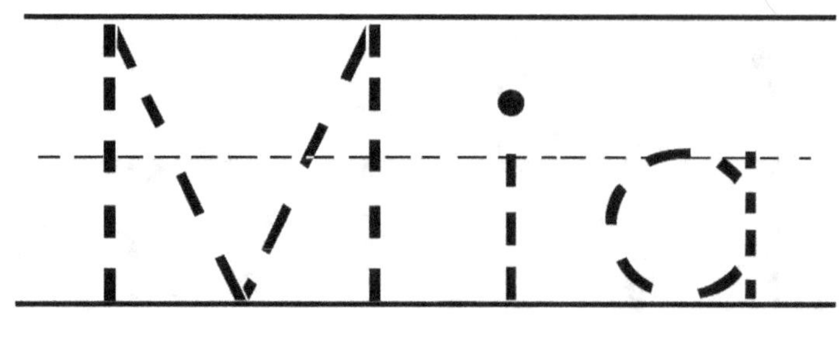

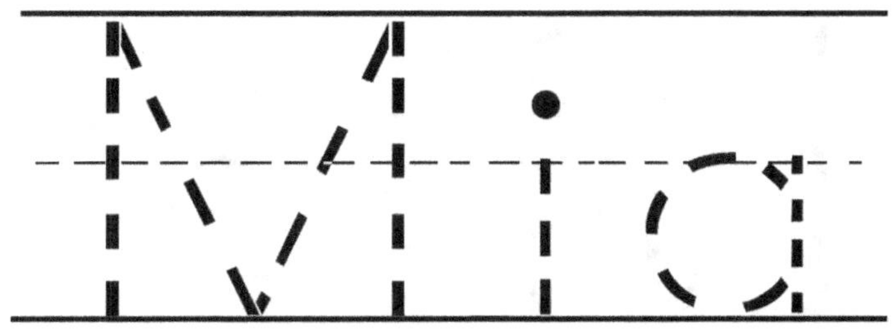

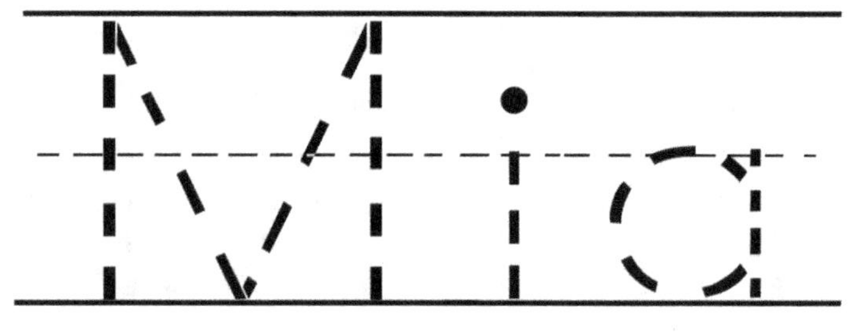

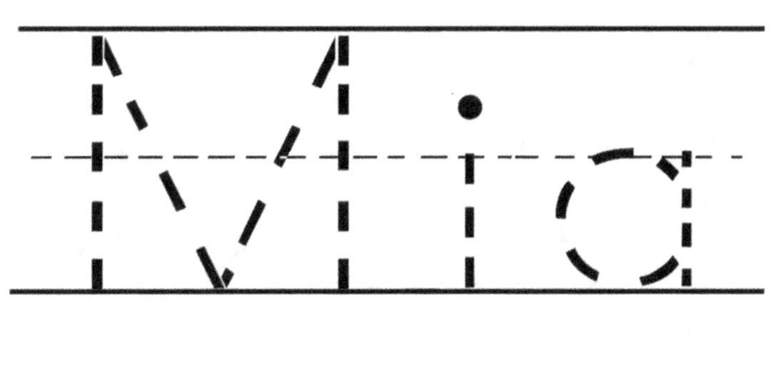
Mia

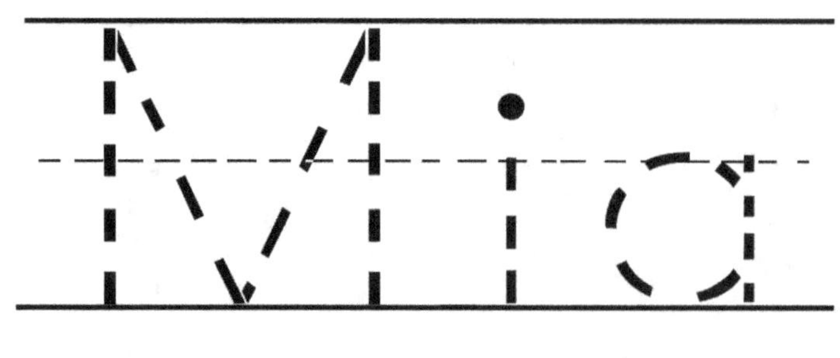

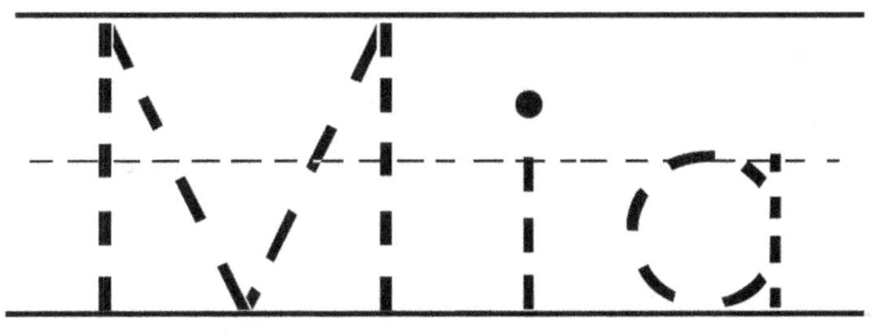
Mia

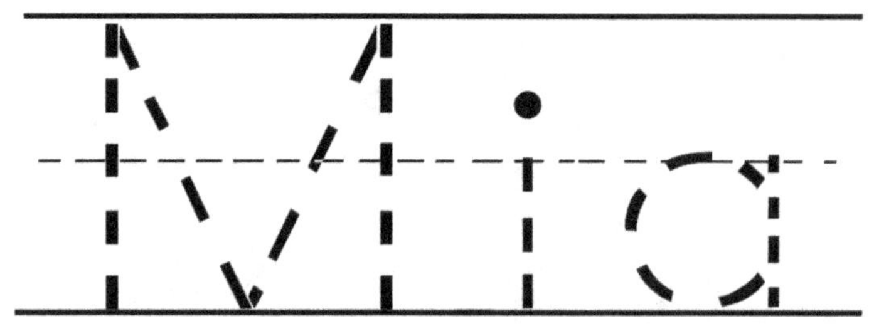

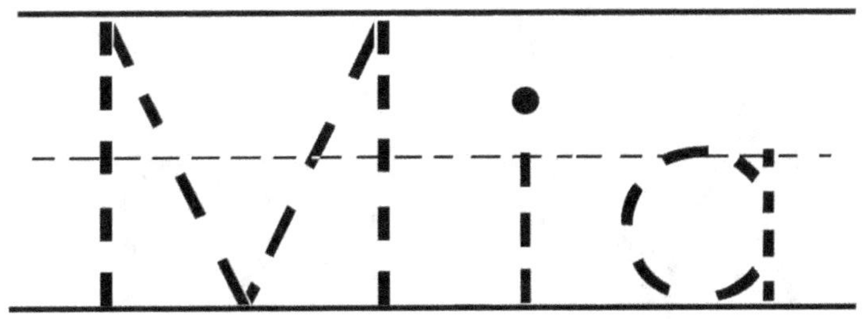

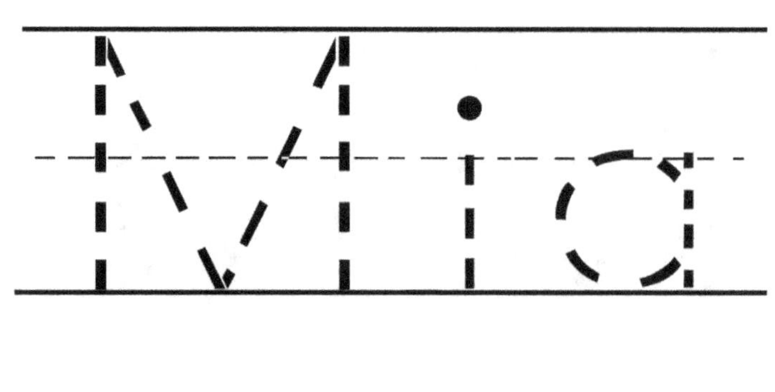

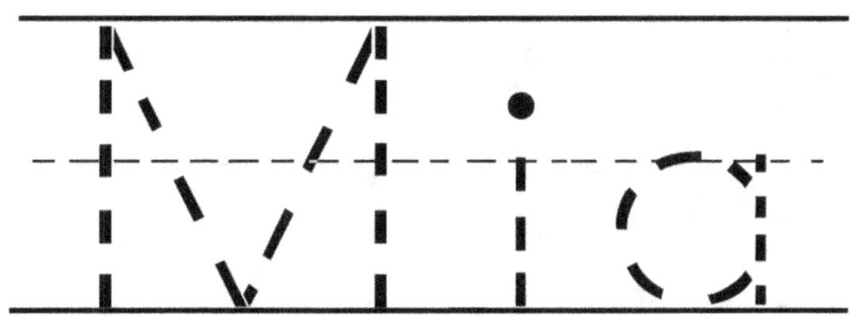

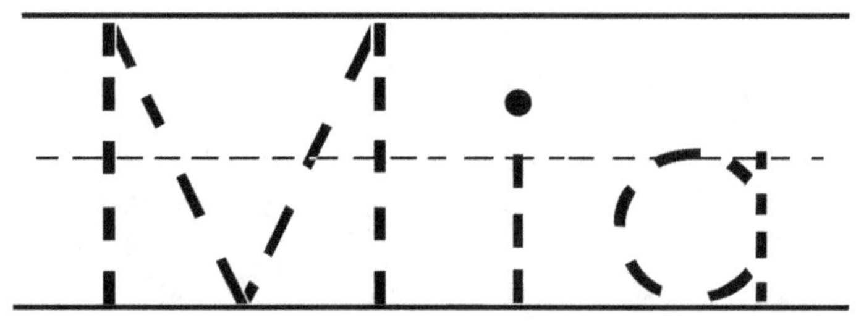

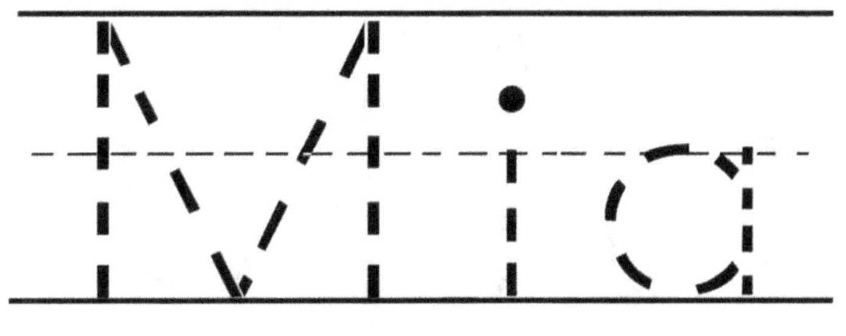
Mia

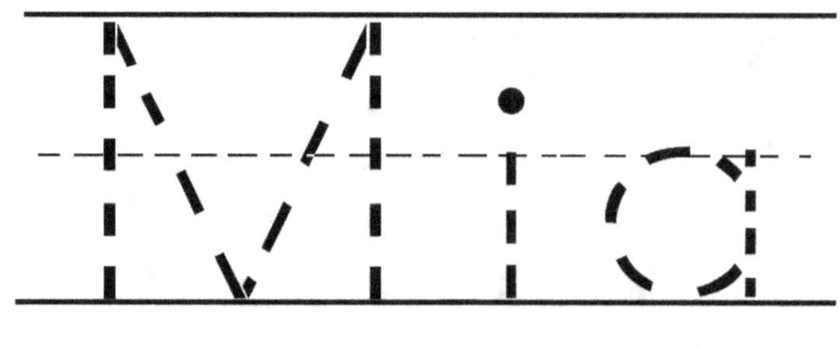

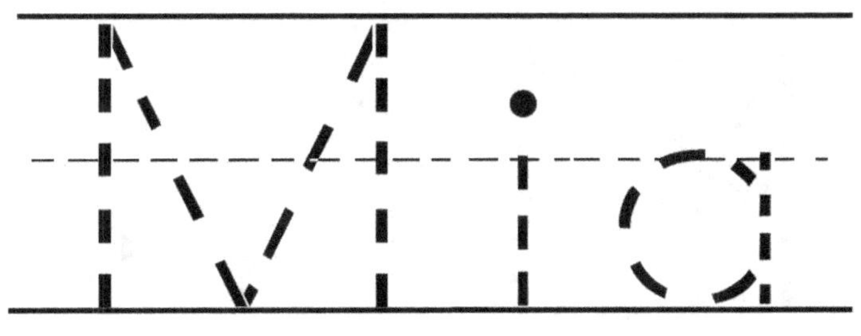
Mia

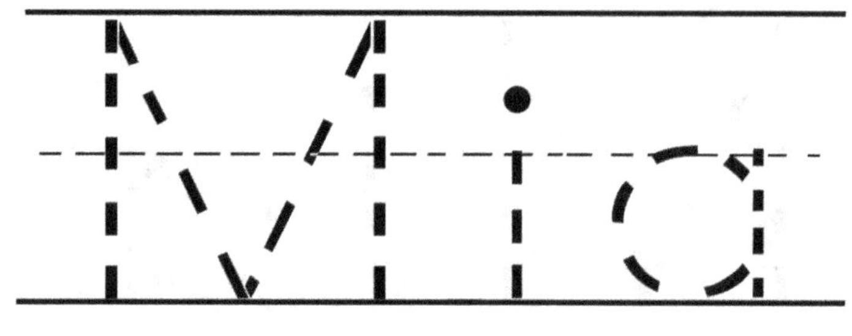

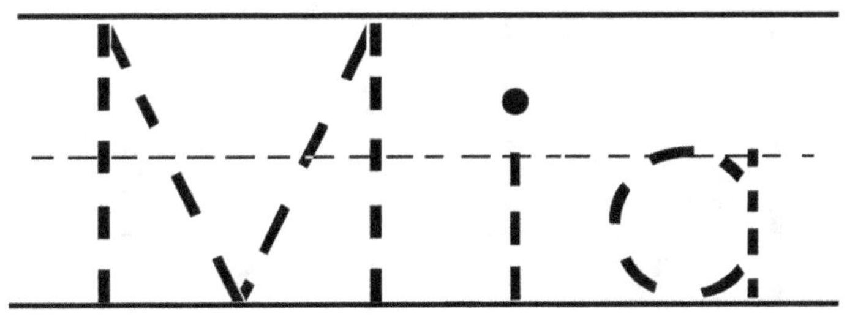

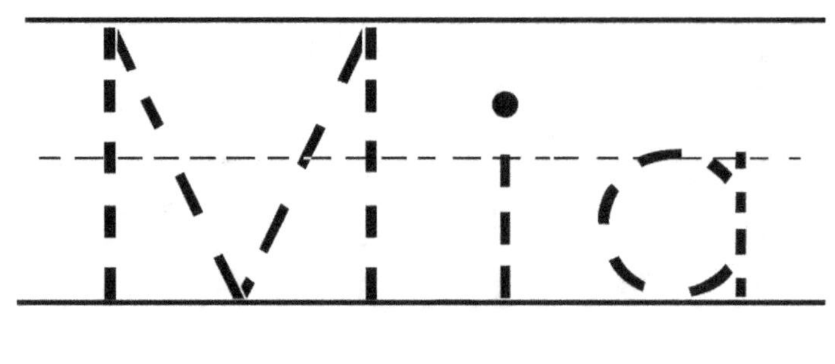
Mia

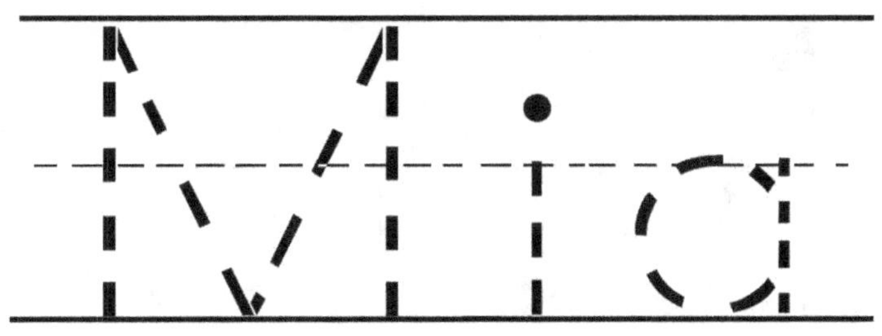

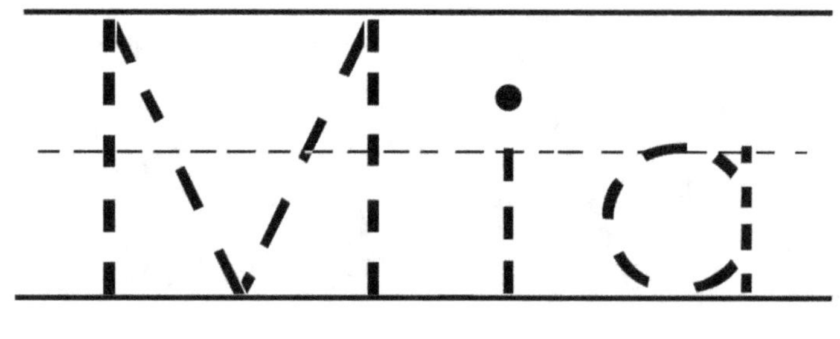

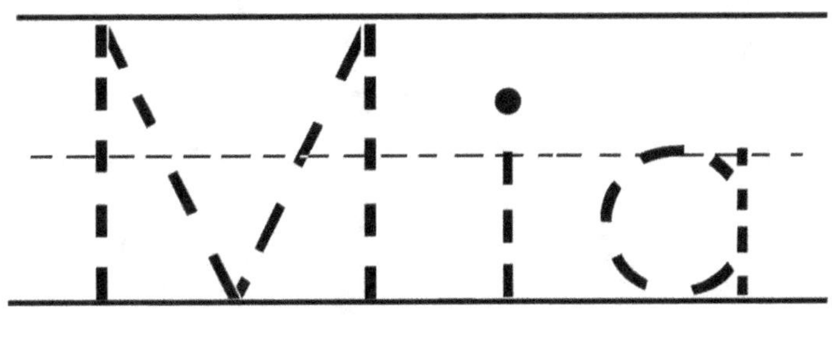

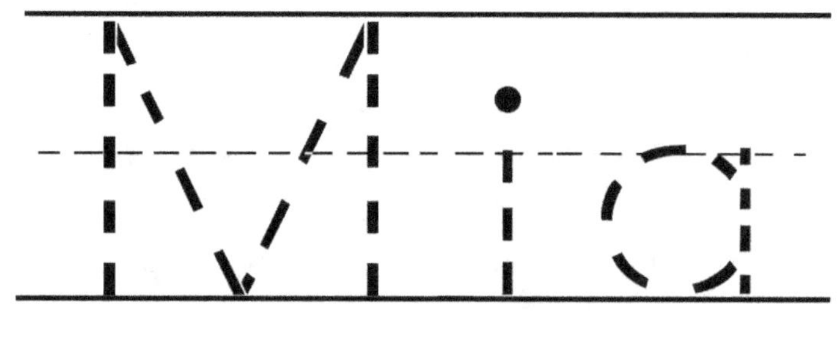

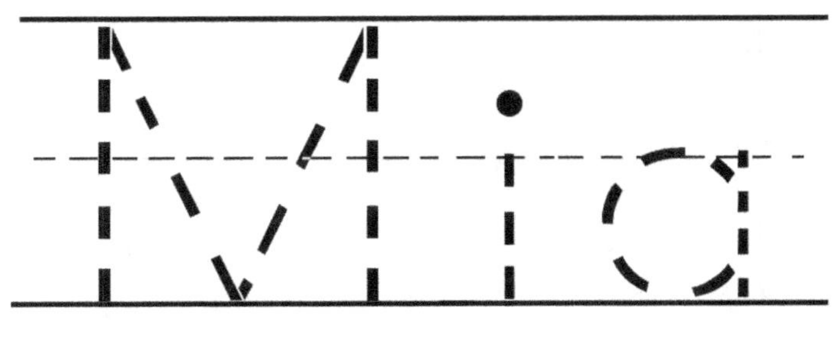
Mia

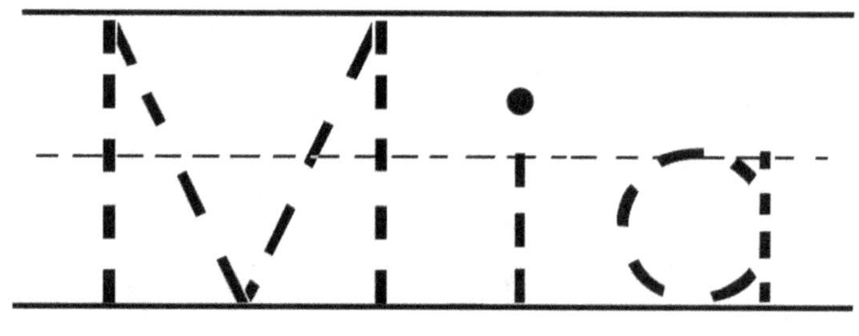

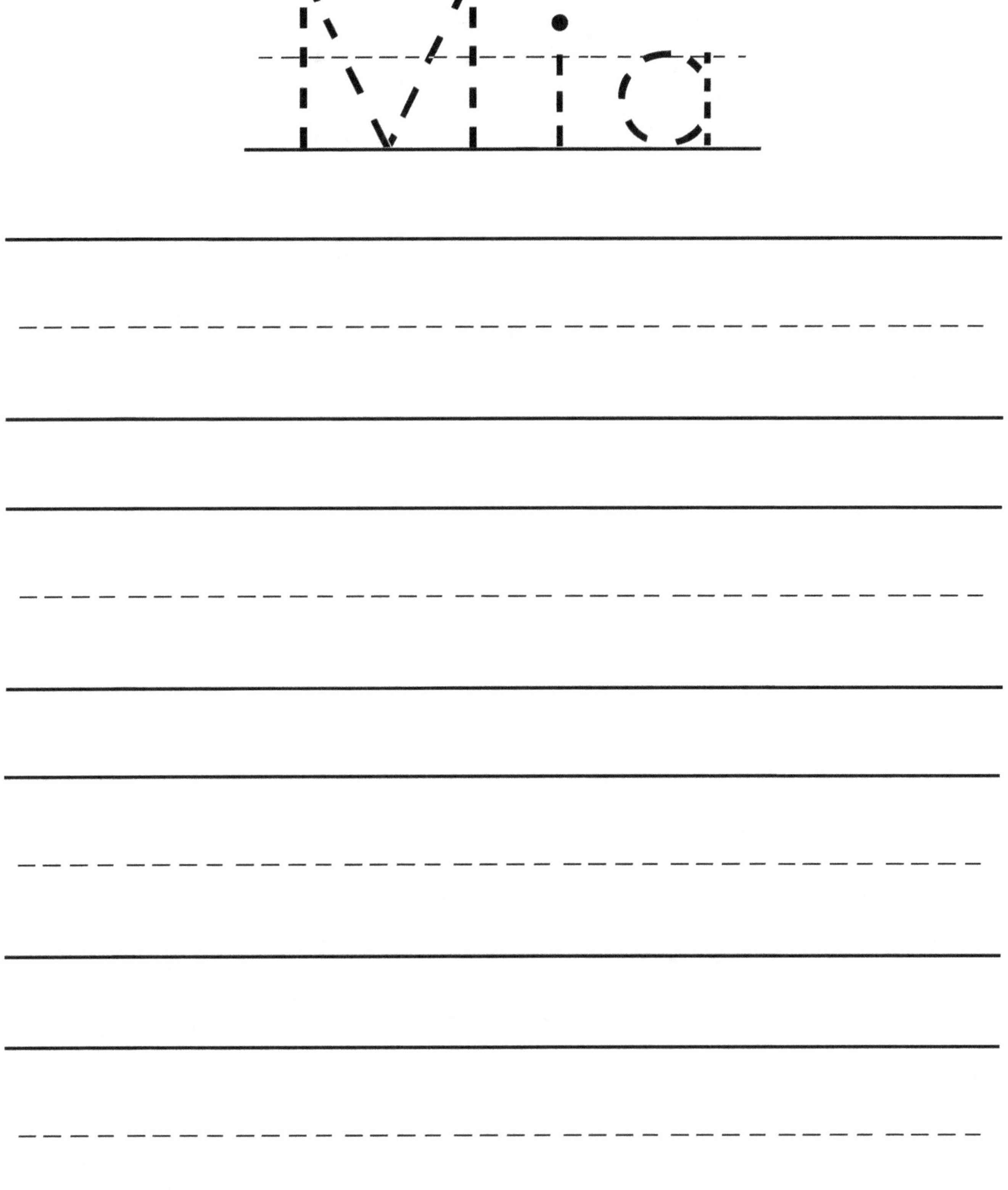

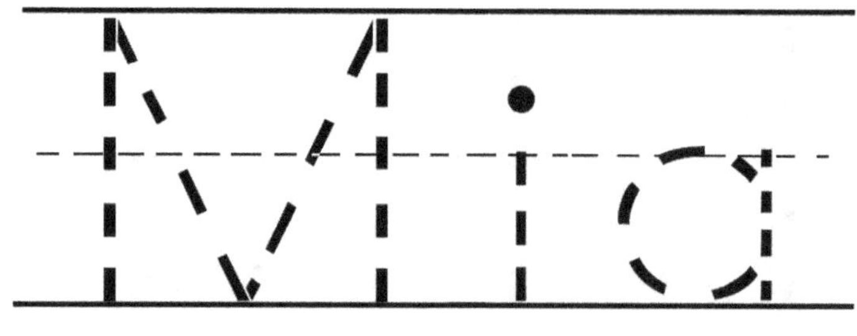

Mia

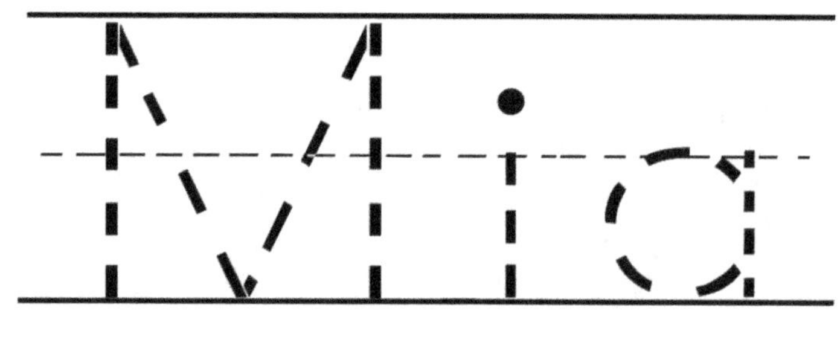
Mia